THE BIG BOOK OF
BARBECUE SIDES

RICK BROWNE HOST OF PUBLIC TELEVISION'S BARBECUE AMERICA

COLLECTORS PRESS

PORTLAND, OREGON

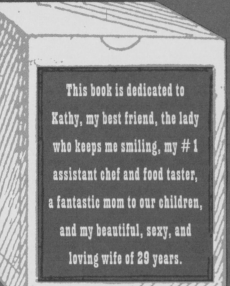

This book is dedicated to
Kathy, my best friend, the lady
who keeps me smiling, my # 1
assistant chef and food taster,
a fantastic mom to our children,
and my beautiful, sexy, and
loving wife of 29 years.

Collectors Press books are available at special discounts for bulk purchases, premiums, and promotions. Special editions, including personalized inserts or covers, and corporate logos, can be printed in quantity for special purposes. For further information contact: Special Sales, Collectors Press, Inc., PO Box 230986, Portland, OR 97281. Toll free: 1-800-423-1848.

For a free catalog write: Collectors Press, Inc., PO Box 230986, Portland, OR 97281. Toll free: 1-800-423-1848 or visit our website at: www.collectorspress.com.

Library of Congress Cataloging-in-Publication Data

Browne, Rick, 1946–
    The big book of barbecue sides / by Rick Browne.
        p.   cm.
    Includes index.
    ISBN 1-933112-17-4 (pbk. : alk. paper)
    1. Cookery, American. 2. Side dishes (Cookery)
    3. Barbecue cookery. I. Title.
    TX715.B894 2006
    641.8'1—dc22   2005031733

Printed in Singapore
First American edition
9 8 7 6 5 4 3 2 1

Design Drive Communications, New York
Managing Editor Lindsay Brown, Collectors Press, Inc.
Editors Rebecca Pepper, Tasia Bernie
Proofreader Jennifer Weaver-Neist .

Distributed by Publishers Group West

Your **free enhanced version** of this book is at www.enhancedbooks.com! Visit today.

193◻311◻21◻74

TABLE OF CONTENTS

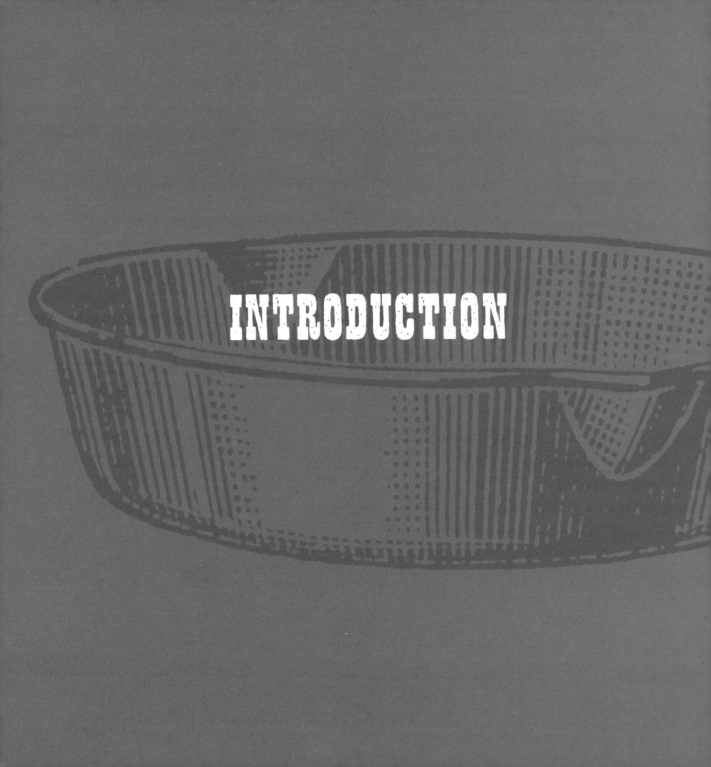

INTRODUCTION

Barbecue,

at least the backyard variety, really began hitting its stride in the 1950s. Visions of Dad popping burgers on a grill, and Mom, bedecked in an apron, whipping up potato salad and her tricolor Jell-O dessert are everywhere in the magazines, newspaper food sections, and even TV programs of that era.

Things were simpler around the grill then, including the food we cooked and ate. About as far as we got with barbecue main dishes was a slab of ribs or half-chickens slathered with store-bought sauce. And there were perhaps three or four sauces to choose from. Sides were standard too, but man were they good!

In the past ten years there has been an incredible change in how America barbecues. The grills themselves now range in price from a couple of hundred dollars to three to four thousand dollars. And we don't just use charcoal anymore but cook with exotic hardwoods and designer mesquite charcoals, with propane and LP (liquid petroleum gas) in the fray now as well.

Our menus are as sophisticated as four-star restaurants as we cook up appetizers that include rare Asian white prawns, mushrooms we'd never heard about ten years ago, and cuts of meat that weren't even in 1950s cookbooks.

But barbecue is back, bigger and better than ever. Whether it's your neighbor grilling a chicken sitting atop a beer can on a kettle grill, the chef at a pricey restaurant tending to a full beef brisket marinated for 24 hours in mustard and spices and then cooked over mesquite and apple chips in a smoker, or you at a beach picnic, drooling over a fancy burger you've doctored with blue cheese and a fiery habanero sauce that's sizzling over an electric grill, barbecues are lighting up America.

Amid this friendly fire and fragrant smoke, folks are trying new dishes to expand their barbeculinary cuisine: juniper berry brined elk roast, grouper stuffed with soft shelled blue crabs; buffalo rib-eyes slathered with imported French butter, blue cheese, and brandy; and other exotic meats like kurabota pork and Kobe beef. We stuff and grill veggies we just learned existed yesterday and are culinary adventurers, going where no human has gone before.

But alongside the chops, steaks, fillets, and roasts are the unsung heroes of barbecue: the side dishes or, as we call them, simply "the sides."

What would a barbecue or picnic be without crisp salads, savory beans, flavorful fruits, pungent grilled breads, bowls of al dente pasta, and fresh-from-the-garden veggies done up right over hot coals? Sure, there are new items here, but this book reflects a distinct rollback to the classic sides we ate with those backyard burgers and dogs: real potato salad with hard-boiled eggs, hand-crafted macaroni and cheese (yes, today made with imported English white Cheddar cheese), and even tricolor gelatin and tomato aspic salads. Retro BBQ is back in full force.

In seven years of pursuing barbecue's holy grail for my public TV series *Barbecue America*, and in researching four previous cookbooks, I've discovered world-class side dishes that truly make any barbecue come alive with vibrant color and mouth-watering flavor. And it's been surprising how many folks are reaching back into family recipe boxes and pulling out heirloom recipes for deviled eggs, green bean casseroles with onion rings, mouth-watering corn puddings, and real, made from scratch dirty rice.

Whether it's a classic creamy coleslaw, a clever new way to grill corn on the cob, a pancake made of spaghetti, or a recipe for the black bean pie that Grandma used to make, I offer here some of the best side dishes I've tasted on my pilgrimage across America's barbecue heartlands, and some I've adapted from Mom's handwritten cooking notes.

Some old, some new, some borrowed, some bleu. I'm proud to present the newest side dishes to hit the tables as well as some old, reliable standards that are making a culinary comeback. I want you to savor the exotic and experimental, alongside the classic dishes that you enjoyed once upon a time at family reunions.

I encourage you to try these recipes, both the new generation and the senior citizens of sides, but also to adapt them to your own tastes. Put in less oregano and more basil, use turbinado sugar instead of brown, try rice vinegar in place of cider vinegar, make a salsa from lychee fruit and star apple and serve it beside a sweet potato pie and a basket of baking powder biscuits. Try your mom's recipe for Waldorf salad along with a 1990s creation of watermelon, goat cheese, and fresh mint. The old and the new—both of them are delicious.

Above all, have fun with these recipes, and let them inspire you to explore even more delicious sides. Go into your closets and pull out the recipes for dishes mom made that you hunger for but forgot how to make. Let *The Big Book of Barbecue Sides* lead you onward to exciting backyard cooking adventures! **ThankQUE, Rick Browne**

CHAPTER 1 SALADS

From traditional standbys to modern classics, salads have always been a welcome addition to any barbecue. Whether you like them creamy, crispy, or tossed, a refreshing salad rounds out the perfect party menu.

Creamy Coleslaw

Coleslaw got its name from the Dutch *koolsla*, simply meaning cabbage (*kool*) salad (*sla*). It became a popular side dish in America after New York City deli owner Richard Hellmann created a bottled mayonnaise, which he began marketing in 1912.

Serves 8

3/4 cup mayonnaise

3 tablespoons sugar

1 1/2 tablespoons white wine vinegar

1/3 cup olive oil

2 tablespoons grated sweet onion, such as Maui, Walla Walla, or Vidalia

1/8 teaspoon dry mustard

1/8 teaspoon celery salt

Dash of black pepper

1 tablespoon fresh lemon juice

1/2 cup half-and-half

2 medium carrots, shredded with a vegetable peeler

1/4 teaspoon salt

1 large head green cabbage, finely shredded

1. In a large bowl, blend together the mayonnaise, sugar, vinegar, and oil. Add the onion, mustard, celery salt, pepper, lemon juice, half-and-half, carrots, and salt, stirring until smooth.

2. Pour the dressing over the shredded cabbage in a large bowl and toss until the cabbage is well coated. Keep refrigerated until ready to serve.

Tip: For a stronger vinegar flavor, reduce the mayonnaise to 2 tablespoons, increase the sugar to 1/4 cup, and increase the vinegar to 1/4 cup.

Twelve-Fruit Salad

Here's a yummy summer salad that not only tastes great but is healthy and good for you. You can substitute any fruits you don't like with those you do, such as raspberries instead of strawberries, or honeydew melon instead of watermelon.

Serves 8 to 10

1 cup fresh lime juice

1/2 cup water

1/2 cup sugar

2 medium nectarines, thinly sliced

1 large firm banana, peeled
and thinly sliced

1 medium tart apple, such as Granny
Smith or Rome Beauty, thinly sliced

1 (11-ounce) can mandarin orange
segments, drained

1 pint blueberries

2 large peaches, pitted and sliced

1 pint strawberries, hulled and sliced

1 1/2 cups seedless watermelon balls

1 cup green seedless grapes

1 cup red seedless grapes

2 medium plums, pitted
and coarsely chopped

2 kiwifruit, peeled and chopped

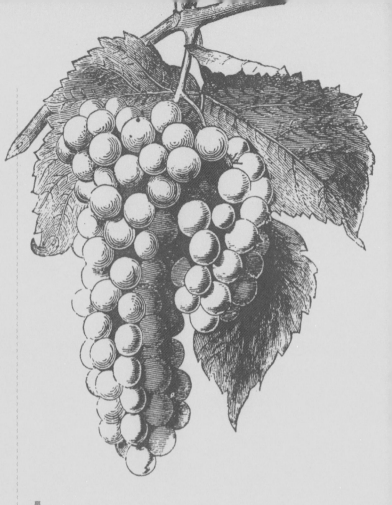

1. In a medium bowl, stir together the lime juice, water, and sugar until the sugar is dissolved. Add the nectarines, banana, and apple and toss to coat.

2. Combine the remaining ingredients in a large bowl, then fold in the nectarines, apple, and bananas.

3. Cover and refrigerate for 1 hour and serve with a slotted spoon.

Tip: You can substitute any of your favorite fruits here, but remember that fruits like pears, apples, or peaches turn brown when exposed to the air. Coating them with the lime juice and sugar will keep them looking fresh.

Carrot Salad

This light and fresh-tasting dish is bright on the taste buds and has almost no calories or fat. Did you know that the first carrots were white, purple, red, yellow, green, and black —not orange?

Serves 4 to 6

1 (1-pound) package baby carrots, shredded in a food processor

3 to 5 scallions, thinly sliced

2 tablespoons fresh lemon juice

2 tablespoons fresh orange juice

2 teaspoons Dijon mustard

1/4 cup olive or peanut oil

Salt and pepper

1. In a medium bowl, toss the carrots and scallions together. Set aside.

2. Mix the juices and mustard together in a small bowl. Whisk in the oil and beat until smooth and well mixed.

3. Pour the dressing over the carrot mixture and toss.

4. Season to taste with salt and pepper and serve cold or at room temperature.

Tip: For some variety try other mustards, including stone-ground grainy, honey-Dijon, raspberry vinaigrette, or sweet onion.

Quick and Easy Coleslaw

This slaw is rich, creamy, and tastes wonderful chilled. Do not let it sit uncovered in the hot sun on a picnic table; keep it in a bowl of ice with a cover over it.

Serves 10 to 12

1 1/2 pounds green cabbage, shredded 1/8 inch thick

2/3 cup sugar

1/3 cup white vinegar

1 teaspoon salt, plus more to taste

1 cup heavy cream

Black pepper

1. Place the cabbage in a large bowl, then cover and refrigerate until well chilled, about 30 minutes.

2. Mix the sugar, vinegar, and 1 teaspoon salt in a small bowl. Add the dressing to the cabbage, tossing well. Add the cream and toss again. Cover and refrigerate for 30 minutes.

3. Season to taste with salt and pepper and serve.

Tip: For more color, shred half a head of red cabbage and half a head of green cabbage and mix together. You can also use a vegetable peeler to shred 2 to 3 carrots and add them to the slaw as well.

Classic

Three-Bean Salad

This classic is great for cookouts or any occasion, and it brings back my summer memories of Niagara Falls visits, watermelon pickles, frosty root beer, cold chicken, and family.

Serves 6

3/4 pound green beans, or 1 (11-ounce) can cut green beans, drained

3/4 pound yellow beans, or 1 (11-ounce) can cut yellow beans, drained

1 (15-ounce) can kidney beans, rinsed and drained

1/2 cup chopped bell pepper (preferably both red and green)

1/2 cup finely chopped sweet onion, such as Maui, Walla Walla, or Vidalia

Dressing:

1/2 cup vegetable oil

1/2 cup cider vinegar

1 teaspoon salt

1/2 teaspoon black pepper

1/2 to 3/4 cup sugar

1. Combine the beans, bell peppers, and onions in a large serving bowl.

2. In a small bowl, whisk together the dressing ingredients; pour over the vegetables. Toss with a spoon to coat well.

3. Cover and refrigerate for at least 8 hours. Serve at room temperature.

Tip: Some people like to add chopped hard-boiled eggs, bacon, or olives to this salad. But I prefer a simpler salad made with fresh green and yellow beans, when possible.

Tennessee Limp Salad

In the rest of the world this is called a limp or wilted salad, but in the South it's often known as "killed salad" because of what happens to fresh garden greens when warm dressing is generously applied.

Serves 4 to 6

6 thick slices bacon

18 cups lettuce of choice, torn into 3-inch pieces

2 cups spinach, torn in half

1 cup butter lettuce, torn into 3-inch pieces

4 scallions, sliced 1/2 inch thick

1/4 cup olive oil

2 tablespoons honey

1/2 teaspoon minced garlic

1/4 cup cider vinegar

Salt and pepper

3 large eggs, hard-boiled, peeled, and sliced

1. Cook the bacon in a frying pan until crispy. Remove from the pan and crumble, reserving the fat in the pan.

2. Use your hands to toss the greens and scallions in a large bowl until well mixed; set aside near the stove.

3. Add the olive oil, honey, garlic, and vinegar to the bacon fat and stir over medium heat until the honey dissolves. Season to taste with salt and pepper.

4. Immediately pour the hot dressing over the salad, and quickly mix. Garnish with the sliced eggs and serve while still warm.

Tip: Serve with hot garlic bread and grilled fruit, such as Jack Daniel's Peachtarines.

Strawberry-Raisin-Pomegranate Salad

This bright and refreshing salad is guaranteed to elicit praise from everyone who tries it. When served on a hot summer day, it seems to melt the heat away, mouthful by mouthful.

Serves 4

1 large head butter lettuce

1 pint strawberries, hulled and sliced

1 cup golden raisins, soaked in warm Marsala wine for 20 minutes

1/2 cup pomegranate seeds

1/2 cup sliced figs

3 ounces blue cheese (preferably Crater Lake Blue)

Salt and pepper

2 tablespoons Marsala wine

1. Distribute the lettuce leaves evenly among 4 salad bowls and refrigerate.

2. In a large bowl, gently mix the strawberries, drained raisins, pomegranate seeds, and figs.

3. Add the cheese and season to taste with salt and pepper. Sprinkle the wine over the top and gently stir to incorporate. Serve in chilled salad bowls.

Tip: If you can't find Crater Lake Blue cheese in the cheese section of your local grocery store, drive to Central Point, Oregon, or save gas by ordering online (www.roguecreamery.com).

Watermelon and Goat Cheese Salad

Looking for a delicious, palate-cleansing, perfectly marvelous salad from down under? This refreshing salad was served to my wife, Kathy, and I on a recent trip to Cairns, Australia. We attended a dinner party hosted by the owner of the internationally known Red Ochre restaurant, where they feature kangaroo, wallaby, alligator, and other local specialties. Good on ya, mate!

Serves 6 to 8

8 cups cubed seedless watermelon (1-inch cubes)

1 cup crumbled goat cheese

2 tablespoons chopped fresh mint

1 teaspoon chopped fresh cilantro

2 tablespoons fresh lemon juice

Mint leaves, to serve

1. Excluding the mint leaves, mix all the ingredients in a large bowl and toss lightly. Refrigerate until ready to serve.

2. Allow the salad to come to just below room temperature (cool but not ice cold), then decorate with mint leaves before serving.

Tip: For a bit more variety and flavor, add 1/2 cup raspberries and 1/2 cup kiwifruit.

Classic Italian Bread Salad

Don't throw away that stale half-loaf of French or Italian bread! Take a cue from the Italians and make a festive bread salad. The flavors are intense, accented heavily by the anchovy and capers. And even folks who think they don't like those two savories will be delighted by the complexity of this wonderful dish.

Serves 8

5 cups cubed leftover French or Italian bread (1-inch cubes)

4 tablespoons red wine vinegar, plus more to taste

2 tablepoons balsamic vinegar, plus more to taste

1/2 cup dry white wine

1 tablespoon anchovy paste,
or 2 anchovies, finely chopped

1/2 teaspoon minced garlic

1 small rib celery with leaves, thinly sliced

2 small yellow bell peppers, seeded
and cut into 1/2-inch pieces

1 small cucumber, peeled, seeded, and diced

2 pounds tomatoes, cut into 1-inch pieces

16 fresh basil leaves

10 fresh mint leaves

4 scallions, cut into 1-inch pieces

1 tablespoon vinegar-marinated capers,
well rinsed

1 medium red onion, thinly sliced

1/4 cup olive oil

3 ounces Parmigiano-Reggiano cheese,
grated (about 1 cup)

Salt and pepper

1. Put the bread in a large serving bowl and
drizzle 2 tablespoons of wine vinegar and
1 tablespoon of balsamic vinegar over it,
mixing well. Pour the white wine over the
bread and again mix thoroughly. Refrigerate
for 30 minutes.

2. In a medium bowl, use a fork to mash the
anchovy paste and garlic together, then mix
in the remaining 2 tablespoons wine vinegar
and 1 tablepoon balsamic vinegar. Let the
mixture sit for 15 minutes.

3. Add the celery, bell peppers, cucumber,
and tomatoes to the anchovy mixture. Chop
the basil and mint leaves, reserving 1 to 2
tablespoons for garnish, and add to the
bowl containing the anchovy-vinegar mixture. Add the scallions, capers, red onions,
and olive oil and stir gently to incorporate.

4. Add the cheese to the bread mixture in the
large bowl. Add the anchovy mixture and
toss to combine. Season to taste with salt
and pepper. Taste and add more vinegar,
if needed. Garnish with the reserved mint
and basil leaves and serve lightly chilled.

*Tip: Some people like to lightly toast the
bread before making the salad. I prefer slightly
stale bread. By adding hard-boiled eggs and
chopped cooked ham, chicken, or shrimp, you
can make this into a main course. You can
also garnish with Kalamata olives.*

Warm German Potato Salad

The tangy flavors of mustard and vinegar in this recipe are softened by sugar and beer, making a sweet-tart flavor that is wonderful with thick slices of ham, grilled sausages like bratwurst, or smoked pork chops.

Serves 6 to 8

1/2 pound sliced bacon

3 pounds waxy potatoes, such as thin-skinned red or white

1/2 cup finely chopped red onion

1/3 cup chopped fresh herbs, such as basil, parsley, chives, and rosemary

Mustard-beer sauce:

2 tablespoons butter

2 tablespoons all-purpose flour

1/2 teaspoon dry mustard

1 tablespoon sugar

1 cup beer

1/2 teaspoon hot pepper sauce, such as Tabasco

2 tablespoons chopped fresh parsley

Salt and pepper

3 large eggs, hard-boiled, peeled, and sliced

1. Cook the bacon until it's crisp and drain on paper towels. Chop the pieces coarsely, place in a medium bowl, and set aside.

2. In a large pot, cook the potatoes in lightly salted water until tender but not mushy. Drain, cool slightly, and slice (unpeeled) into thick rounds. Return to the empty pot.

3. While the potatoes are still warm, gently mix in the reserved bacon, onions, and herbs. Set aside.

4. In a large bowl, mix up the mustard sauce by combining all the sauce ingredients. Add the potato-bacon-herb mixture while gently stirring.

5. Season to taste with salt and pepper, garnish with the eggs, and serve warm.

Tip: This salad is even better the second day. Rewarm before serving.

American Potato Salad

Truly a classic recipe, this potato salad has graced millions of barbecues and picnics over the years. The tender but not mushy potatoes blend perfectly with the vinegar, mustard, hard-boiled eggs, mayonnaise, and sweet pickles for a delicious blend of textures and flavors.

Serves 6

2 pounds red potatoes

2 tablespoons red wine vinegar

1/2 teaspoon salt

1/2 teaspoon black pepper

5 large hard-boiled eggs, peeled

1 small rib celery, finely diced

1/4 cup diced sweet pickles
(not relish; 1/4-inch dice)

3 scallions, thinly sliced or diced

2 tablespoons chopped fresh parsley

1/2 cup mayonnaise

2 tablespoons prepared or Dijon mustard

Dash of paprika

1. Place the potatoes in a large pot with enough water to cover. Bring to a boil, cover, and simmer, stirring to ensure even cooking, until tender, 25 to 30 minutes.

2. Drain, rinse under cold water, and drain again. Place in the freezer for 15 minutes.

3. Cut the cooled potatoes into 3/4-inch cubes with a serrated knife. Layer them in a wide, shallow bowl and season with the vinegar, salt, and pepper.

4. Chop 3 eggs and place in a small bowl with the celery, pickles, scallions, and parsley. Mix well and add to the potatoes.

5. Stir in the mayonnaise and mustard and gently turn the mixture over with a rubber spatula until everything is combined.

6. Chill, covered, before serving. Slice the remaining 2 eggs. Sprinkle the salad with the paprika, garnish with the egg slices, and serve.

Tip: Waxy, moist potatoes, like the red ones used here, have a lower starch content and higher sugar content than baking potatoes, making them "stickier" and best for boiling or for making scalloped potatoes and potato salad.

Sweet Bean and Corn Salad

Room temperature beans from a can? Yes, they make a delightful, tasty salad to serve with burgers, hot dogs, or grilled ribs. The pineapple and mandarin oranges add a tangy touch.

Serves 4 to 6

1 (28-ounce) can baked beans (preferably Bush's Original)

1 (16-ounce) can kidney beans, rinsed and drained (preferably Bush's)

1 (16-ounce) can garbanzo beans, rinsed and drained (preferably Bush's)

1 (15.2-ounce) can corn, drained

1/2 cup pineapple juice

1 (8-ounce) can mandarin orange segments, drained

2 tablespoons balsamic vinegar

Pinch of ground cinnamon

1. Mix all the ingredients in a large saucepan. Stir gently and cook until the beans are hot and the liquid barely begins to bubble.

2. Serve hot or at room temperature with your favorite grilled meat or fish dish.

Tip: Add additional fruit if desired. Chopped peaches, apples, or nectarines do well in this salad.

Classic Cucumber and Dill Salad

If you're in the mood for a light, cool dish that's perfect on a hot summer day, this is the one for you. The dill actually adds nutritional benefits to a mostly non-nutritional vegetable.

Serves 4 to 6

2 to 3 medium cucumbers, peeled and thinly sliced

Salt

1/3 cup sour cream

1 tablespoon vinegar

1 1/2 tablespoons chopped fresh dill

Black pepper

1. Arrange the cucumber slices in a serving bowl, sprinkling each layer with salt. Place a saucer or other weight on the cucumbers to weigh them down. Cover and let stand for several hours.

2. In a small bowl, combine the sour cream, vinegar, and chopped dill and season to taste with the pepper.

3. Pour off the cucumber juices from the bowl and add the sour cream mixture. Mix well with a spoon and serve chilled.

Tip: For those who don't like cucumber seeds, cut the peeled cucumbers in half lengthwise and scoop out the seeds with a spoon. Chop the cucumber into bite-size pieces and proceed with the recipe as instructed.

Classic
Northern Coleslaw
with Apples

This is a typical coleslaw from north of the Mason-Dixon Line, utilizing a couple of different seasonings and the sweet bite of apples.

Serves 6 to 8

1/2 cup sour cream

1/2 cup mayonnaise

1 tablespoon fresh lemon juice

2 teaspoons celery seeds

1 teaspoon sugar

1/4 teaspoon salt

Dash of black pepper

4 cups (3 cups green, 1 cup red) shredded cabbage (about 1 pound)

3 medium tart apples, such as Granny Smith or Pippin, peeled, cored, and thinly sliced

1. In a large bowl, combine the sour cream, mayonnaise, lemon juice, celery seeds, sugar, salt, and pepper; mix well.

2. Add the cabbage and apple slices and toss lightly until completely coated. Serve immediately.

Tip: If making an hour or two in advance, add the apple slices just before serving. I like to use a tart apple, but any variety works well.

Deviled Eggs

This recipe has been in my family for more than fifty years, and when served at picnics, the eggs disappear within seconds. The tang of the mustard and vinegar, the smooth blend of egg yolks and mayonnaise, and the slight hint of sweetness create a winning combination.

Serves 6

6 extra-large eggs

1 teaspoon prepared mustard

1 teaspoon cider vinegar

3 tablespoons mayonnaise

1 teaspoon sugar

1/2 teaspoon salt

1/8 teaspoon black pepper

Paprika, to serve

1. Place the eggs gently in a medium saucepan. Add cold water until it is 1/2 inch above the tops of the eggs. Cover with a lid and heat quickly to a boil. Immediately turn the heat off, cover, and let sit for 20 minutes.

2. Place the hot pan in the sink and run very cold water over the cooked eggs until cool enough to handle, or put the eggs in ice water. Tap the eggs lightly all over and peel under cold running water. Cut each egg in half lengthwise, removing the yolks carefully and putting them in a small bowl.

3. Mash the yolks with a fork and add the mustard, vinegar, mayonnaise, sugar, salt, and pepper. Mix well.

4. Carefully spoon the mixture into the hollow of the eggs, and sprinkle the tops with paprika. Place the eggs in a single layer on a platter. Cover and keep refrigerated until ready to serve.

Tip: Lots of folks boil the heck out of hard-boiled eggs and then find a black line around the yolk when they cut them open. Bringing them to a boil and then turning off the heat and covering the pan stops the discoloration. The cold water and ice make them easy to peel.

Classic
Green Pea and Beet Salad

A surprise awaits you with this salad! The first time I had it, I couldn't believe the combination, but I went back for seconds. Using fresh beets that have been boiled just until they begin to soften makes all the difference—as does using fresh garden peas.

Serves 4 to 6

1 pound (6 medium) beets, boiled, trimmed, peeled, and diced, or 2 (15-ounce) cans diced beets, drained

2 cups peas

6 large hard-boiled eggs

1 large onion, diced

2 medium ribs celery, diced

3/4 cup mayonnaise

1 tablespoon sugar

Leaves lettuce of choice, to serve

1. Chill the beets and peas overnight.

2. Peel the cooled eggs, transfer to a medium bowl, and chop coarsely. Mix in the onions and celery and set aside.

3. In a medium saucepan, boil the peas just until tender. Set aside to drain and cool.

4. Put the beets in a large bowl and gently stir in the peas. Add the egg mixture, mayonnaise, and sugar and mix well.

5. Place individual lettuce leaves on plates and serve with a scoop of salad on each.

Tip: Use thawed frozen peas if you don't have fresh peas, though freshly shelled peas are far superior in texture and taste.

Tomato Aspic

In my family, this molded tomato dish was as traditional as turkey on Thanksgiving and Christmas. The mold is secured with gelatin, which dates back to the Middle Ages, when cooks discovered that a thickened meat broth could be made into a jelly to seal cooked meat and keep it from spoiling. Centuries later, with a little creativity and tweaking, aspic was born!

Serves 4 to 6

3 envelopes unflavored gelatin

3 cups cold tomato juice

2 cups tomato juice, heated to boiling

1/4 cup fresh lemon juice

2 tablespoons sugar

1 1/2 teaspoons Worcestershire sauce

1. Sprinkle the gelatin over 1 cup of cold tomato juice in a large bowl and let stand for 1 minute.

2. Add the heated tomato juice and stir until the gelatin is completely dissolved, about 5 minutes.

3. Stir in the remaining 2 cups cold tomato juice, lemon juice, sugar, and Worcestershire sauce.

4. Pour into a 5 1/2-cup ring mold or bowl and refrigerate until firm, about 4 hours. Serve chilled.

Tip: My mother sometimes used vinegar instead of lemon juice for a sharper flavor.

Cracker Salad

This classic southern dish sounds unusual but tastes wonderful. Serve it with fried chicken, country fried steak, fried fish, pot roast, or barbecue, accompanied by a fresh, chilled mint julep. This recipe was shared with me by Janet Wells, the devoted daughter-in-law of the late, fabulous southern cook Mary "Tot" Wells.

Serves 4 to 6

1 medium green bell pepper, seeded and chopped

3 large red tomatoes, chopped

1 medium onion, chopped

1 large hard-boiled egg, peeled and chopped

Salt

Black pepper

Pinch of sugar, or to taste

1 tablespoon cider vinegar, or more to taste

6 to 8 saltine crackers, crumbled

2 to 3 tablespoons mayonnaise, or more to taste

1. Mix the bell pepper, tomatoes, onion, and egg in a nonreactive bowl. Add salt, pepper, and sugar to taste and let sit for 10 minutes. Drain off any liquid that settles in the bottom.

2. Add the vinegar, enough saltines to soak up the liquid, and mayonnaise. Serve cool or slightly warm.

Tip: The bowl of peppers, tomatoes, onion, and egg can be kept in the refrigerator until ready to serve.

CHAPTER 2 BREADS

There is nothing like fresh bread to tempt your taste buds. We smother it in butter and jam, or simply use it to sop up the juices from our plates. The versatility of bread has made it a staple at our tables through the centuries, any time of year.

Gilroy, California, Garlic Bread

Gilroy, California, is the garlic capital of the universe—the only place where you can hang a steak outside on a clothesline to marinate in the garlic fumes from nearby fields and processing plants. This bread is loaded with garlic flavor, has a wonderful consistency, and is guaranteed to keep vampires away.

Serves 4 to 6

1 package (2 1/2 teaspoons) active dry yeast

1/4 cup warm water

1 cup cottage cheese (preferably small curd), warmed

6 cloves garlic, finely chopped

1 large egg

1 tablespoon olive oil

1 tablespoon dried oregano

2 teaspoons sugar

1 teaspoon garlic or onion salt

1/2 teaspoon baking soda

2 1/2 cups all-purpose flour

1. Soften the yeast in the water in a large bowl.

2. Add the cottage cheese, garlic, egg, oil, oregano, sugar, salt, and baking soda and stir well.

3. Add the flour to the mixture, blend well, and put in a warm place to rise, loosely covered, until doubled in size.

4. Stir the dough down and turn out into a well-greased, 2-quart casserole dish. Let rise for another 30 minutes. Preheat the oven to 350°F.

5. Bake the bread for 40 minutes, or until the top is lightly browned, then let rest for 10 minutes. Slice and serve warm.

Tip: If you wish, you can add some chopped fresh parsley, savory, or basil (1/2 teaspoon each) for a tasty garlic-herb bread.

Yorkshire Pudding

By Jove! The British know a thing or two about roast meat and the best way to eat it—medium-rare served with large portions of Yorkshire pudding (actually more a popover than a pudding) and creamy horseradish on the side.

Serves 6

4 large eggs

1 1/2 cup sifted all-purpose flour

2 cups milk

1/4 teaspoon garlic powder

1/2 teaspoon dried savory

Salt and pepper

Drippings from 1 standing rib roast of beef or 1 crown roast of pork or 1 rack of lamb, straight from the oven or barbecue

1. Shortly before the roast finishes cooking, beat the eggs with a fork in a small bowl.

2. Add the eggs to the flour in a large bowl and beat with a wooden spoon until elastic. Gradually add the milk, whisking until smooth. Add the garlic and savory, and season with salt and pepper to taste. Set aside.

3. When the roast has reached its desired doneness, take it out of the pan you've cooked it in and let it stand on a deep plate, covered in aluminum foil, to let the juices return to the center of the meat. Do not turn off the oven.

4. Set the oven temperature to 450°F. Return the roasting pan to the oven and heat until the drippings are almost smoking.

5. Remove the pan from the oven and use a brush to coat the insides of the pan with the hot grease all the way to the top.

6. Pour the batter into the pan and return to the oven for 25 to 30 minutes, until the pudding is crisp and brown on the outside but still soft and moist on the inside. The batter will have risen up the sides of the pan like a popover.

7. Immediately cut the pudding into squares and serve alongside the roast meat.

Tip: Instead of cooking the pudding in one pan, you can put 1 tablespoon of hot drippings in each cup of a 6-cup muffin pan. Brush it up the sides of the cups, return to the oven, and heat to smoking. Pour 1/4 cup of batter into each cup and bake the same as the large pan. Check carefully for when the puddings are puffed up and turning brown, and remove from the oven.

Genoa, Italy, Garlic Juice Bread

Italians love their garlic bread. To make this garlicky bread even more pungent with the stinking rose, rub a fresh clove of garlic over each slice after the first toasting, and then add the flavored butter. *Mama mia—* that's garlic bread!

Serves 4 to 6

1/2 cup (1 stick) butter

2 to 3 teaspoons garlic juice

6 to 8 slices French bread

1. Melt the butter in a small saucepan and stir in the garlic juice.

2. Lightly toast the French bread.

3. Place the pieces of bread on a baking sheet and brush the melted butter-garlic mixture on each. Preheat the broiler.

4. On a rack positioned 2 to 3 inches under the broiler, lightly toast the bread pieces until the tops are slightly bubbly. Watch carefully to avoid burning. Serve immediately.

Tip: If your local supermarket doesn't carry bottled garlic juice, you can purchase it online from www.garlicvalleyfarms.com or www.madeincalifornia.net.

Onion Focaccia

If you love onions and other members of the onion family, this dish is right up your alley. The only member not used here is leeks, and those could easily be added if you wish. This bread is onion-sweet and has a nutty, herbal flavor. Serve by itself or spread with a fresh tomato sauce or salsa.

Serves 4 to 6

1 package (2 1/2 teaspoons) active dry yeast

1/2 teaspoon sugar

1 cup warm water

3 1/2 cups all-purpose flour

1/2 teaspoon garlic salt

2 tablespoons chopped chives

6 tablespoons olive oil

1 large sweet onion, such as Maui, Walla Walla, or Vidalia, thinly sliced

1 large red onion, thinly sliced

1 large shallot, thinly sliced

4 scallions, finely chopped

1/4 teaspoon crumbled dried sage

1/4 teaspoon dried oregano

Black pepper

1 tablespoon grated Parmesan cheese

1 teaspoon coarse or kosher salt,
or more to taste

1. In the bowl of an electric mixer fitted with the paddle attachment, dissolve the yeast and sugar in the water for 5 minutes, or until the mixture is foamy. Add the flour, salt, chives, and 3 tablespoons of oil, and mix well.

2. With the dough hook attachment, knead the dough for 2 minutes, or until soft and slightly sticky.

3. Form the dough into a ball with your hands, transfer to an oiled bowl, and roll around to coat thoroughly with the oil. Let the dough rise, covered with plastic wrap, in a warm place for 1 1/2 hours, or until doubled in size.

4. Press the dough evenly into an oiled 10 1/2 x 15 1/2 x 1-inch jelly roll pan and let rise in a warm place, covered loosely, for 1 hour, or until it is almost doubled in size again.

5. In a large bowl, stir together the remaining 3 tablespoons oil, onions, shallot, scallions, sage, oregano, and pepper to taste.

6. Preheat the oven to 400°F. Make deep indentations in the dough with your fingers and sprinkle the onion mixture evenly over the top. Follow with a sprinkling of cheese and salt, then bake in the bottom third of the oven for 35 to 45 minutes, or until golden brown.

7. Let the focaccia cool in the pan on a rack and serve warm or at room temperature.

Tip: You can also prepare this dough in a bread machine if all the ingredients are mixed together in advance—including the onion mixture. Do not sprinkle the onions into the bread machine, as they will all fall to the bottom and burn during the cooking process. Bake in a loaf pan, following the directions for your particular machine.

Southern Skillet Cornbread

In the United States and Canada, we've known about and eaten cornbread since the recipe was borrowed from the folks who already lived here when Europeans came ashore. This cornbread is hearty and can be served with roast game, poultry, or beef. Don't serve it with light fish dishes, as it will overwhelm them.

Serves 4 to 6

2 cups coarse yellow cornmeal

1/2 cup all-purpose flour

1 tablespoon sugar

1 tablespoon brown sugar

1 tablespoon baking powder

1 teaspoon salt

1/2 teaspoon baking soda

2 cups buttermilk

2 large eggs, lightly beaten

2 tablespoons melted butter

2 cups fresh, frozen, or canned corn (drain if using canned)

2 teaspoons vegetable oil

1. Preheat the oven or grill to 450°F.

2. In a medium bowl, sift together the cornmeal, flour, sugars, baking powder, salt, and baking soda. Add the buttermilk, eggs, and butter and stir until just mixed. Mix in the corn kernels.

3. Pour the vegetable oil into a seasoned, 10 1/2-inch cast iron skillet and place in the oven, heating until the oil is very hot. Remove the pan from the oven and pour off any excess oil.

4. Pour the batter into the hot skillet and return to the oven. Reduce the temperature to 400°F and bake for 25 to 30 minutes, until the cornbread is golden brown. When done, a toothpick inserted into the center will come out clean.

5. Cool the cornbread in the pan on a wire rack for 5 minutes. Invert it onto a large plate, cut into thick wedges, and serve.

Tip: Tangerine butter goes great with this bread. Mix 1/4 cup (1/2 stick) very soft butter with the juice of 1 tangerine, 1/2 teaspoon grated tangerine zest, 1 tablespoon curaçao, and 2 teaspoons confectioners' sugar. Chill and serve with the cornbread.

Cape Cod Cheese and Corn Muffins

Asiago cheese adds a surprising texture and zip to these scrumptious muffins. Or you could add Huntsman, blue, or other strong cheese to create the same effect. People in the East love their corn muffins so much that the schoolchildren of Massachusetts began a petition drive to establish the corn muffin as a staple of New England cooking. The Massachusetts legislature agreed and made it the official state muffin.

Makes 12

3/4 cup all-purpose flour

2 1/2 teaspoons baking powder

3/4 teaspoon salt

1 tablespoon sugar

1/2 cup coarse yellow cornmeal

1 cup grated Asiago cheese (about 3 ounces)

1 large egg, beaten

3/4 cup milk

2 tablespoons shortening, melted and cooled

1. Preheat the oven to 400°F.

2. Combine the flour, baking powder, salt, and sugar in a medium bowl and stir in the cornmeal and cheese.

3. Make a well in center of the flour mixture and add the beaten egg, milk, and melted shortening. Stir just until the dry ingredients are moistened.

4. Grease the cups in a 12-cup muffin pan and fill each two-thirds full with the batter.

5. Bake for 20 to 25 minutes, or until nicely browned. Serve warm or at room temperature.

Tip: You can also use a more traditional, grated cheese, such as Cheddar, Jack, or Swiss.

Classic
Baking Powder Biscuits

Serve these golden biscuits with fresh butter, homemade strawberry or apricot jam, and a piping hot cup of tea. If you have any left over, they are wonderful when covered in country sausage gravy.

Makes 12 biscuits

2 cups all-purpose flour

2 teaspoons baking powder

1/2 teaspoon salt

1/4 cup butter or shortening

3/4 cup milk

1. Preheat the oven to 400°F.

2. Into a large bowl, sift the flour once. Measure and adjust as necessary to make 2 cups. Add the baking powder and salt and sift again.

3. Cut in the butter using your hands, a pastry cutter, or a fork.

4. Add the milk gradually, stirring until a soft dough is formed. Turn out onto a lightly floured board and lightly knead for 30 seconds, enough to form a ball.

5. Roll the dough out 1/2 inch thick and cut with a 2-inch floured biscuit cutter. You should be able to make 12 biscuits.

6. Place the biscuits on an ungreased baking sheet and bake for 12 to 15 minutes, or until browned. Serve warm.

Tip: You can also make tiny tea biscuits with a small cutter or the rim of a small glass.

Mighty Fine Biscuits

Arguably the greatest and most delicious comfort food of all time is indescribably flaky and mouth-watering biscuits topped by decadently rich and creamy sausage gravy. (I didn't say healthy, I said delicious.) This variety is yeast-raised, which requires a bit more time but is well worth the wait.

Makes 24 biscuits

1 package (2 1/2 teaspoons) active dry yeast

1/4 cup warm water

2 cups buttermilk, at room temperature

5 cups all-purpose flour

3 tablespoons sugar

1 tablespoon baking powder

1 teaspoon baking soda

2 teaspoons salt

3/4 cup shortening

1. In a small bowl, dissolve the yeast in the warm water. Let stand until creamy, about 5 minutes, then add the buttermilk and set aside.

2. In a large bowl, mix the flour, sugar, baking powder, baking soda, and salt. Cut in the shortening with a pastry blender until the mixture resembles coarse meal or flakes. Stir in the yeast mixture until moistened. Turn the dough out onto a lightly floured surface, and knead 4 or 5 times.

3. Roll the dough out to 1/2-inch thickness and cut out biscuits with a 2 1/2-inch floured biscuit cutter. Place the biscuits on lightly greased baking sheets so they are barely touching each other. Cover and let rise in a warm place for 1 hour, or until almost doubled in size.

4. Preheat the oven to 425°F. Bake for 10 to 12 minutes, or until browned. Serve warm.

Tip: If you have leftover biscuits, use them for breakfast. Fry 1 pound bulk sausage until crumbly. Season to taste with salt and pepper. Stir in 1 tablespoon sugar and brown for about 1 minute. Stir in 3/4 cup all-purpose flour, then slowly stir in 4 cups milk and continue to stir until thickened. Serve the gravy hot over the biscuits.

Spicy Pineapple Fritters

These fritters are a great side dish with sliced ham, roast beef, and thick pork chops. Serve them instead of a starch, with collard greens, black-eyed peas, or sautéed squash.

Serves 4 to 6

2 cups cake flour

1/3 cup sugar

1/2 tablespoon baking powder

1/2 tablespoon baking soda

1/2 tablespoon salt

1 cup milk

1 large egg, lightly beaten

1 teaspoon vanilla extract

1/4 cup pineapple juice

1 cup chopped and drained pineapple

1/2 cup chopped scallions

1/4 teaspoon cayenne pepper

Vegetable oil, for frying

Paprika, to serve

1. To make the batter, sift the flour, sugar, baking powder, baking soda, and salt into a large bowl. Make a well in the center and add the milk, egg, vanilla, and pineapple juice. Mix gently with a fork until all the ingredients are incorporated; do not overmix.

2. Combine the pineapple and onions in a small bowl, and fold into the batter. Sprinkle the cayenne pepper over the top.

3. In a cast iron Dutch oven or large, heavy skillet, heat the oil to 370°F. Using an ice cream scoop, drop scoops of batter into the hot oil and fry until deep golden brown.

4. Use a slotted spoon to remove the fritters from the fryer and drain on paper towels. Sprinkle with paprika and serve.

Tip: You can use other fruit to make fritters, such as peaches, nectarines, and bananas. Use fruit essence instead of the juice in the batter, and use chopped fruit in the base.

Citrus and Buttermilk Hushpuppies

Hushpuppies are a staple in the South, and not many barbecue meals are served without them. There's a bit of Florida sunshine in these to give you an orange-lemon flavor that wakes up the cornmeal.

Serves 6 to 8

2 cups coarse yellow cornmeal

1 cup all-purpose flour

3/4 teaspoon seasoned salt

1/2 teaspoon black pepper

1 teaspoon baking powder

1/8 teaspoon baking soda

2 tablespoons brown sugar

2 large eggs, lightly beaten

1 tablespoon corn or olive oil

1 1/2 cups buttermilk

1/4 cup heavy cream

1/4 cup lemonade

2 tablespoons grated orange zest

Oil, for frying

1. Mix the cornmeal, flour, salt, pepper, baking powder, baking soda, and brown sugar in a large bowl. Add the eggs, oil, buttermilk, cream, lemonade, and orange zest and stir until thoroughly blended into a thick batter. Cover and set aside.

2. Heat 3 inches of oil in a Dutch oven to 350°F. Use a tablespoon to drop spoonfuls of batter into the hot oil.

3. Allow the batter to brown on all sides, 2 to 3 minutes per side.

4. Hushpuppies should begin floating when done, but do not overcook them if they do not. They are ready when golden brown all over.

5. Use a slotted spoon to remove the hushpuppies from the oil, and drain on paper towels. Serve warm.

Tip: You can substitute orange, lime, pineapple, tangerine, or grapefruit juice for the lemonade.

Blue Ribbon Blueberry Muffins

One taste of these muffins and you will be magically transported back to your grandmother's house for a Sunday morning breakfast, where Grandma keeps piling fresh-from-the-oven muffins on your plate until you are ready to burst.

Makes 18 muffins

1/2 cup (1 stick) butter, softened

1 cup plus 1 tablespoon sugar

2 large eggs

1 teaspoon vanilla extract

2 teaspoons baking powder

1/4 teaspoon salt

2 cups all-purpose flour

1/2 cup milk

2 1/2 cups blueberries

1. Preheat the oven to 375°F. Grease 18 muffin cups or fill them with paper baking cups.

2. In a medium bowl, whisk the butter until creamy. Add 1 cup of sugar and whisk until the mixture is fluffy and light yellow.

3. Add the eggs one at a time, mixing well with a spoon after each is added. Add the vanilla extract, baking powder, and salt and stir until incorporated.

4. Fold in half of the flour with a rubber spatula, then add half of the milk. Mix well.

5. Add the remaining flour and milk, mix well, and gently fold in the blueberries.

6. Fill the muffin cups two-thirds full with the batter, then sprinkle the tops with sugar. Bake for 25 to 30 minutes, or until the muffins are golden brown.

7. Cool for 15 to 20 minutes before removing from the pan and serving.

Tip: You can substitute other berries like raspberries, blackberries, huckleberries, or other favorites. Just be very gentle when adding them so the berries are not crushed, leaking juices into the batter.

Boston Brown Bread

There is nothing like a slice of fresh, warm Boston brown bread with a serving of Boston baked beans. The chewy, sweet bread, full of molasses flavor and plump raisins, is a perfect accompaniment to the rich, smoky beans.

Serves 4 to 6

2 cups all-purpose flour

2 cups whole wheat flour

2 cups coarse yellow cornmeal

2 teaspoons baking soda

1 teaspoon salt

1 1/2 cups dark molasses

1 1/2 cups raisins

3 1/2 cups buttermilk

1. Preheat the oven to 325°F.

2. Sift the flours, cornmeal, baking soda, and salt into a large bowl and mix well.

3. In a medium bowl, stir the molasses and raisins together. Add the buttermilk, stirring until the mixture is smooth.

4. Add the liquid ingredients to the dry ingredients and stir until there are no lumps.

5. Grease a clean, empty 28-ounce can. Line the bottom with wax paper, fill two-thirds full with the dough, then cover with aluminum foil and tie tightly with string.

6. Place the can in a deep baking pan and fill the pan with boiling water, to come halfway up the side of the can.

7. Place in the oven and allow to steam for 2 hours, checking the water level after 1 hour. Add more boiling water if needed. Check by sticking a bamboo skewer into the bread; it will come out clean when done. Remove the string and foil and allow the bread to cool for 1 hour before unmolding.

8. Cut into 1/2-inch-thick slices and serve.

Tip: You can also use smaller cans; simply divide the dough into smaller portions. A 15-ounce can is perfect for two people. Make two and freeze one loaf.

Savory Onion Pudding

Probably the most popular side dish I ever prepared on my TV series *Barbecue America*, this recipe came from my mother's Canadian cookbook. It combines lots of flavors and textures and is the king of comfort foods. Serve with roast beef or pork, grilled leg of lamb, or roast turkey (to replace the stuffing).

Serves 6 to 8

8 tablespoons (1 stick) butter

1 tablespoon olive oil

8 cups thinly sliced onions

1/4 cup dry vermouth

1 clove garlic, crushed

6 ounces French bread, cut into large (2-inch-square) chunks

Sea salt

Black pepper

2 cups shredded Emmental or Swiss cheese (about 8 ounces)

3 large eggs

2 cups half-and-half

1. Preheat a grill or smoker to approximately 350°F. (On a gas grill, turn all the burners on high, then turn down to medium-high when you put the bread in the barbecue.)

2. Melt 4 tablespoons of butter with the oil in a large cast iron pot. Add the onions, cover, and steam over low heat for 15 minutes.

3. Uncover the pot, increase the heat to medium, and cook, stirring occasionally, until the onions caramelize and turn brown. Pour in the vermouth and boil until the liquid evaporates, stirring the whole time.

4. Spray the sides and bottom of a cast iron pan thoroughly with nonstick cooking spray.

5. In a large bowl, mix the garlic, bread, and onions together, stirring well. Spread in the cast iron pan.

6. Melt the remaining 4 tablespoons butter and pour over the bread-onion mixture. Sprinkle with the salt, pepper, and cheese.

7. In a medium bowl, beat the eggs slightly with a fork and add the half-and-half. Pour evenly over the bread and cheese, using a spoon to make sure the liquid is infused into the bread mixture.

8. Bake in the grill, using the indirect heat method, for 30 to 40 minutes, until puffed and golden. If you wish, you can place a

water pan under the cast iron pan at same level as the coals. This keeps the stuffing moist and prevents the bread from sticking to the pan.

9. Remove from the heat, cut into large wedges, and serve.

Tip: Some people prefer the crusts cut off, but I like the difference in texture between the soft bread and pudding and the occasional bit of crunchy crust. You can also use your favorite cheeses instead of those suggested here.

Classic Sweet Potato Biscuits

Nothing tastes as good as a warm biscuit right from the oven, and these southern heritage biscuits are as good as they get. Serve with fresh, creamy butter and maybe a dab or two of peach preserves or raspberry jam. They'll add flair to a meal of fried chicken, grilled ham, or catfish stew.

Makes 12 to 14 biscuits

2 tablespoons butter

1 1/2 cups all-purpose flour

1 1/2 cups cake flour

1 tablespoon baking powder

1 teaspoon salt

1 1/2 cups baked, mashed sweet potatoes

1/4 cup brown sugar

2 large eggs, beaten

1. Preheat the oven to 425°F.

2. Melt the butter in a small saucepan, and set aside to cool.

3. Sift the flours, baking powder, and salt into a medium bowl. Set aside.

4. In a large bowl, stir the butter into the mashed potatoes, blending well. Add the sugar and beaten eggs and stir well to blend. Add the dry ingredients, 1 cup at a time, and blend well to form a dough. Turn out onto a floured board and knead briefly.

5. Roll the dough out to 1/2-inch thickness, then use a 2-inch floured biscuit cutter to cut out the biscuits, placing them on a lightly greased baking sheet. Gather the scraps, form into a ball again, and roll out to 1/2-inch thickness. Continue doing this until all the dough is used; there should be 12 to 14 biscuits.

6. Bake for 15 to 20 minutes or until golden, and serve warm.

Tip: You can also boil the sweet potatoes, but baking gives them a bit more flavor.

CHAPTER 3 PASTA

Pasta is always a wonderful addition to your table. It's filling, colorful, and works well with a wide range of sauces and seasonings. Its versatility ensures boundless ways to complement just about any grilled food.

Spicy Macaroni and Cheese

This creamy, tangy recipe can be baked in the oven or in your barbecue over indirect heat. Either way, the onion soup and two cheeses add a flavor that is indescribable.

Serves 4 to 6

1 (10 1/2-ounce) can cream of onion soup

1/2 cup water

1 1/2 cups shredded Cheddar cheese (about 6 ounces)

3 cups elbow macaroni, cooked

1 tablespoon finely chopped pimento

2 tablespoons chopped sweet onion, such as Maui, Walla Walla, or Vidalia

1 tablespoon finely chopped chives

1/4 cup buttered bread crumbs

1 teaspoon butter, melted

1/2 cup crumbled Huntsman cheese (including the Stilton cheese layer)

1. Preheat the oven or grill to 350°F.

2. Combine the soup, water, Cheddar cheese, and macaroni in a 1 1/2-quart casserole dish. Stir in the pimento, onion, and chives and bake for 30 minutes, or until hot.

3. In a small saucepan, sauté the bread crumbs in the butter until all the butter is absorbed. Set aside.

4. Top the macaroni mixture with the crumbled Huntsman cheese and bread crumbs and bake for 5 more minutes, or until the cheese melts. Serve hot.

Tip: Huntsman cheese is an English cheese available in most cheese shops and major grocery stores. It comprises layers of Stilton (blue) cheese between layers of Double Gloucester cheese.

Fried Ravioli with Italian Green Sauce

Here's an unusual way to prepare pasta and a unique sauce to go with it. The crisp, fried pasta and refreshing sauce make it a great accompaniment for Italian sausage, roast lamb, or barbecued chicken. Make sure you allow enough time for the sauce to stand before serving.

Serves 4 to 6

Italian green sauce:

1 slice French bread, crust removed

2 tablespoons red wine vinegar

1 cup olive oil

1 cup minced fresh parsley

1/4 cup minced red onion

1 large egg, hard-boiled, peeled,
and finely chopped

1 teaspoon minced garlic

4 anchovy fillets, minced

1/2 teaspoon salt

1/4 teaspoon crushed red pepper flakes

2 large eggs

1/2 cup evaporated milk

1 cup dry Italian-style bread crumbs

1/4 cup olive oil

24 small cheese- or spinach-filled ravioli,
thawed if frozen

1/2 cup grated Parmesan cheese

1. To make the green sauce, soak the bread in the vinegar, then crumble it into a medium bowl. Add the vinegar, oil, parsley, onion, chopped egg, garlic, anchovies, salt, and red pepper flakes and stir well. Let stand for 20 minutes before using.

2. In a small bowl, beat the eggs and milk with a fork. Put the bread crumbs in another small bowl and set both bowls aside.

3. In a medium saucepan, heat 1/4 cup olive oil until a drop of water sizzles when dropped in.

4. Dip the ravioli in the egg mixture to coat, letting the excess drip off. Dip them in the bread crumbs, knocking off the excess, and arrange on a baking sheet. (These can be prepared in advance and refrigerated until ready to use.)

5. Fry the ravioli in the oil until they are just turning golden brown.

6. While the ravioli are still hot, sprinkle with Parmesan cheese and serve with Italian Green Sauce as a dip.

Tip: Make your own seasoned bread crumbs by adding herbs to panko, or dry Japanese bread crumbs. Grind the bread crumbs in a food processor along with 2 teaspoons each of dried oregano and basil per cup of bread crumbs. Mix in 1 teaspoon grated Parmesan cheese, and you're set.

Tomato-Basil Bowtie Pasta

The combination of tomato, basil, and pasta is a simple, yet timeless and distinct delight. And since basil comes in so many flavorful varieties, it's up to you to select one for this dish. Try a bit of lemon basil, cinnamon basil, or anise basil for a surprising flavor addition.

Serves 4 to 6

Chicken or vegetable stock

1 (8-ounce) package bowtie pasta

16 ounces cottage cheese

2 cups chopped tomato

1 tablespoon chopped fresh chives

1 tablespoon plus 1 teaspoon olive oil

1/2 teaspoon dried oregano

1/4 teaspoon lemon pepper

1/4 cup finely minced fresh basil

2 ounces mozzarella cheese, cut into 1/2-inch cubes

1. Cook the pasta in chicken or vegetable stock for 7 to 9 minutes, or until soft but still slightly chewy (al dente), stirring often.

2. Mix the cottage cheese, tomato, chives, 1 tablespoon olive oil, oregano, and lemon pepper in a small bowl and set aside.

3. Remove the pasta from the heat, drain well, then return to the cooking pot, adding 1 teaspoon olive oil and stirring to coat all the pasta.

4. Pour the cottage cheese mixture into the pot and stir gently to incorporate all the ingredients.

5. At the last minute, stir in the basil and mozzarella cheese and serve immediately.

Tip: Basil plants are abundant producers, often making it necessary to preserve some for later use. One method is to puree the leaves with a bit of water or oil; portion this into ice cube trays and freeze. When solidly frozen, store the cubes in the freezer in a resealable plastic bag

Sun-Dried Tomato Spaghetti Pancake

Kids love this side dish. It's spaghetti, which they love, cooked in a cool new way. Serve the spaghetti sauce in a pitcher to complete the experience.

2 large eggs

2 tablespoons finely minced onion

1/2 teaspoon dried oregano

1/2 teaspoon salt

1/8 teaspoon black pepper

3 1/2 cups leftover cooked spaghetti, cold

3 tablespoons butter

2 tablespoons grated Parmesan cheese

1 (26-ounce) jar spaghetti sauce

1. Beat together the eggs, onions, oregano, salt, and pepper together in a medium bowl.

2. Add the spaghetti; toss well to coat. Heat 2 tablespoons of butter in a medium skillet over moderate heat until the foam subsides. Add the spaghetti mixture and sprinkle with the cheese. Cook until the bottom is lightly browned. Turn out onto a plate.

3. Heat the remaining tablespoon of butter in the pan. Slide the spaghetti pancake back into the pan, uncooked side down. Cook until lightly browned. Cut into serving pieces, and serve.

Tip: You can also use other pastas, especially fettuccine, angel hair pasta, and other long, thin pastas that bind well in the pan, to form the pancake shape.

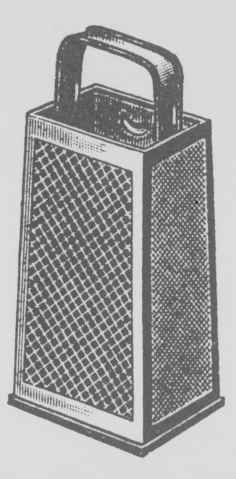

Pasta and Bean Soup (Pasta e Fagioli)

Fagioli translates from Italian to English as "beans," and there are hundreds of pasta e fagioli recipes using every type of bean known to man, including kidney, lima, navy, pinto, fava, black-eyed pea, black bean, and green bean. So you can substitute your favorite legume here if you wish.

Serves 6

1 pound fresh or canned Great Northern beans (rinsed and drained if using canned)

1 cup canned pinto beans, rinsed and drained

5 quarts water, plus more as needed

1 (6-ounce) can tomato paste

1 1/2 tablespoons salt

1 teaspoon dried basil

1 teaspoon dried oregano

2 1/2 tablespoons granulated garlic, or 1 1/2 tablespoons garlic powder

1 medium rib celery, finely chopped

1 cup olive oil

6 medium carrots, finely chopped or grated

1/2 pound small shell macaroni

Grated Parmesan cheese, to serve

1. In a deep stockpot, cook the beans in the water for 15 minutes, boiling the water hard until the beans sink.

2. Add the tomato paste, salt, basil, oregano, garlic, celery, oil, and carrots and stir, then keep a slow, rolling boil going for 15 to 20 minutes, or until the beans are soft but not mushy.

3. If the soup is too thick, add a little more water, 1/2 cup at a time.

4. In another deep pot, cook the macaroni in salted water until soft but still slightly chewy (al dente), about 5 minutes.

5. Drain the macaroni well, and add to the soup just before bringing it to the table. Sprinkle some Parmesan cheese over each bowl and serve.

Tip: This soup should be 70 percent soup and 30 percent pasta.

German Noodles, Peas, and Cabbage

A recipe given us by a German housekeeper, this is classic comfort food. Neither fancy nor complicated, it just tastes real good and is easy to fix. There are never any leftovers.

Serves 4 to 6

1 (12-ounce) package wide egg noodles

1 tablespoon margarine or butter

1 tablespoon olive oil

1 large onion, thinly sliced

1 medium savoy cabbage, ribs removed, thinly sliced,

1/4 teaspoon black pepper

1/2 teaspoon salt

1 teaspoon fresh thyme leaves, or 1 teaspoon dried savory

1 (10-ounce) package frozen peas

1 cup chicken stock

1/4 cup grated Parmesan cheese, plus more to serve

Chopped fresh parsley, to serve

1. Heat a large saucepan of salted water to boiling over high heat, then add the noodles and cook until soft but still slightly chewy (al dente), about 7 minutes.

2. In a nonstick 12-inch skillet, heat the margarine and oil over medium heat until melted and sizzling. Add the onions and cook for 15 minutes, or until tender and beginning to brown, stirring occasionally.

3. Increase the heat to medium-high and add the cabbage, pepper, salt, and thyme, and cook, stirring occasionally, for 5 minutes, or until the cabbage is tender-crisp and golden.

4. Stir in the frozen peas and the stock and cook for 2 to 3 minutes, stirring constantly.

5. Drain the noodles and return to the saucepan. Immediately add the cabbage mixture and the Parmesan cheese, and toss well to coat.

6. Serve in a heated bowl, with parsley and Parmesan cheese sprinkled on top.

Tip: In a pinch for a quick veggie for the barbecue? Quarter a cabbage, remove the core, put the wedges on a sheet of aluminum foil, drizzle melted butter over each, add salt and pepper, seal the foil, and cook for 15 minutes over hot coals, turning once. Voila —a tasty veggie, and nutritious too!

Twice-Browned Noodles

Also called "both sides browned" noodles, these are popular in Shanghai, where there are noodles stands on many streets. By adding grilled shrimp, fish, chicken, or pork, you can make this into a full meal.

Serves 4 to 6

1 pound wide egg noodles

1 tablespoon sesame oil

3 tablespoons peanut or vegetable oil, or more as needed

1/4 cup slivered scallions

1/4 cup slivered red bell peppers

Salt and pepper

Grated Parmesan cheese, to serve

Chopped fresh parsley, to serve

1. In a large saucepan, add enough water to cover the noodles and bring to a boil.

2. Add the noodles, stirring to separate, and cook until soft but still slightly chewy (al dente), 7 to 10 minutes. Drain thoroughly and rinse with cold water. Drain again and toss with the sesame oil.

3. In a large, heavy frying pan or wok, heat 3 tablespoons peanut oil over medium-high to high heat.

4. In a large bowl, gently mix the scallions and red peppers with the noodles until thoroughly mixed.

5. Add the noodles to the frying pan and season to taste with salt and pepper. Quickly spread the noodles out to the edges of the pan, and cook, without stirring, until browned on the bottom, 5 to 8 minutes.

6. Flip the noodles over and brown the other side. Transfer to a plate and keep warm in the oven until ready to serve.

7. Just before serving, sprinkle with Parmesan cheese and parsley.

Tip: You can also add straw mushrooms or julienned portobello mushrooms when you are mixing the noodles, peppers, and scallions.

Armenian Noodle Casserole

Big on cheese? Then this dish is for you, combining three cheeses into a comfort food casserole that will fill you up and please the palate at the same time. If you like, you can add crumbled sausage or chopped bacon for a little more protein.

Serves 6

1 pound lasagna noodles

1/4 cup (1/2 stick) butter, melted

2 cups very thinly sliced onion

1 pound Monterey Jack cheese, shredded (about 4 cups)

1 cup small-curd cottage cheese

1 cup ricotta cheese

1/4 cup finely chopped fresh chives

2 large eggs, well beaten

1 cup chopped fresh Italian parsley

1/2 teaspoon garlic salt

1 teaspoon white pepper

1. Preheat the oven to 350°F.

2. Cook the lasagna noodles in boiling salted water until soft and pliable (see the Tip).

3. Lightly brush a 9 x 9-inch baking dish with some of the melted butter and line with a layer of the cooked noodles. Add a layer of paper-thin onion slices.

4. In a medium bowl, mix the cheeses, chives, eggs, parsley, garlic salt, and white pepper together and then spoon a layer of this filling over the noodles. Add another layer of noodles and onions and another layer of the cheese mixture, repeating until you run out of ingredients. Make sure the last layer is noodles.

5. Brush the remaining butter on top of the noodles and bake until golden brown.

6. Cut into 3-inch squares and serve hot or cold.

Tip: Because the pasta in lasagna is cooked twice—boiled first and then combined with other ingredients and cooked in the oven—pasta in baked dishes should boil for less time than normal. Cook the lasagna noodles until just flexible but still quite firm (usually about one-third of the normal cooking time).

Creamy Vegetable Fettuccine

Classic

This pasta side dish is super with barbecued or oven-roasted chicken. Feel free to add or subtract veggies you don't like or would prefer to use: halved Brussels sprouts instead of the broccoli, green beans instead of the peas, zucchini instead of the carrot, and so on. If you prefer, serve the sauce over cooked white rice instead of fettuccine.

Serves 6

1 (12-ounce) package fettuccine

1 tablespoon olive oil

2 cups broccoli florets

1 cup diced celery

1 cup diced carrot

1 large onion, diced

2 cloves garlic, finely chopped

3/4 teaspoon dried basil

1 (12-ounce) can evaporated milk

1 cup grated Parmesan cheese

1/8 teaspoon black pepper

3/4 teaspoon dried savory

2 tablespoons cornstarch

1 cup chicken stock

1 cup thinly sliced red bell pepper

1/2 cup fresh or frozen peas

1. Cook the fettuccine in a pot of salted boiling water until soft but still slightly chewy (al dente), about 7 minutes. Drain and keep warm.

2. Heat the olive oil in a large skillet over medium-high heat. Add the broccoli, celery, carrot, onions, garlic, and basil and cook, stirring occasionally, for 5 minutes, or until the vegetables are tender.

3. Stir in the evaporated milk, 1/4 cup of Parmesan cheese, pepper, and savory and bring to a boil. Reduce the heat immediately to low and cook, covered, for 5 minutes.

4. Combine the cornstarch and a small amount of stock in a small bowl, then stir into the skillet. Gradually stir in the remaining stock, and add the bell pepper and peas.

5. Cook over medium heat, stirring constantly, until the sauce is thickened and the vegetables are tender, being careful not to boil.

6. Pour the sauce over the warm fettuccine, sprinkle with the remaining Parmesan cheese, and serve.

Tip: There are more than 500 different pasta shapes, with names that are descriptive but not particularly appetizing: worms, little boys, little ears, small mustaches, radiators, little tongues, autumn leaves, butterflies, twins, thimbles, bridegrooms, and ribbons. Fettuccine is recommended here, but the cheese sauce could be served over any pasta variety.

Classic
Macaroni Salad

This is a classic macaroni salad recipe, made with hard-boiled eggs and slivers of scallions. I remember this from picnics in Canada when my Aunt May and Uncle George would bring a huge wooden bowl full of it to every family reunion.

Serves 4

1/2 pound elbow macaroni

1/2 cup finely diced celery

3 tablespoons chopped fresh parsley

3 hard-boiled eggs, peeled and chopped

1/4 cup thinly sliced scallions

1/2 cup mayonnaise

2 teaspoons prepared mustard

3/4 teaspoon salt

1 teaspoon sugar

1/2 teaspoon dried basil

1/4 teaspoon black pepper

Chopped fresh parsley, to serve

1. Cook the macaroni in boiling salted water according to the package directions, then drain.

2. In a large bowl, combine the macaroni, celery, parsley, chopped eggs, and scallions. Toss gently.

3. Combine the mayonnaise with the mustard, salt, sugar, basil, and pepper in a small bowl, and stir into the macaroni thoroughly.

4. Refrigerate until ready to serve, then garnish with parsley.

Tip: For color and added taste, you can add chopped pickles; red, green, and yellow bell peppers; and even olives.

Classic Macaroni and Cheese

This is the homemade version of an American favorite: smooth, cheesy macaroni that is soaked in flavor. According to *The Dictionary of American Food and Drink*, macaroni and cheese was first made in the nineteenth century, but it took on an even greater popularity when Kraft Foods introduced its macaroni and cheese dinner in 1937. Kraft now sells more than one million boxes of these dinners every day!

Serves 4 to 6

1/2 pound elbow macaroni

6 tablespoons butter

1/4 cup all-purpose flour

1 teaspoon salt

1/2 teaspoon dry mustard

1/4 teaspoon black pepper

3/4 teaspoon Worcestershire sauce

3 cups milk

1 small onion, grated

3 cups shredded sharp Cheddar cheese (about 3/4 pound)

3/4 cup soft bread crumbs

1. Preheat the oven to 375°F. Cook the macaroni in a pot of salted boiling water according to the package directions, drain, and keep warm.

2. In a medium saucepan, melt 4 tablespoons of butter over medium-low heat; blend in the flour, salt, dry mustard, pepper, and Worcestershire sauce, stirring until smooth and bubbly.

3. Gradually stir in the milk; cook and stir until thick and smooth.

4. Stir in the grated onion and cheese.

5. Place the macaroni in a buttered 3-quart casserole, then pour the sauce over it and gently mix to blend.

6. Melt the remaining 2 tablespoons butter and toss with the bread crumbs.

7. Sprinkle the bread crumbs over the macaroni and bake for 30 minutes, or until golden brown.

Tip: For a tasty variation, try using different pastas, pumpernickel bread, and Swiss cheese, or mix several cheeses, like Swiss, Cheddar, and a pinch of blue cheese.

Southwestern Pasta Salad

My dear friend Susan Foley, shared this classic recipe, which she mixes up for tailgate parties. The crunchy kernels of corn, the smooth pasta, and the buttery avocados add up to a wonderful side dish that goes great with quesadillas or grilled chicken tacos.

Serves 6

1/2 pound conchiglie pasta, large elbow macaroni, or penne

1 medium sweet onion, such as Maui, Walla Walla, or Vidalia

2 medium tomatoes

2 medium avocados, peeled and pitted

2 ears corn with husks

1 bunch fresh cilantro, finely chopped

1/3 cup canola oil

Juice of 1 lime

Salt and pepper

1. Cook the pasta in heavily salted water according to the package directions and drain.

2. Coarsely chop the onion, tomatoes, avocados, and cilantro, mix in a large bowl, and set aside.

3. Grill or microwave the corn in moistened husks until done. If grilling, turn the ears when the bottom husks are well browned, then keep turning until all sides are browned. If microwaving, put the ears in a resealable plastic bag, add 1 tablespoon water, close partway, and cook on high for 7 minutes.

4. Cut the kernels off the ears.

5. Add the corn to the bowl of vegetables and add the cooked pasta, canola oil, and lime juice. Toss to mix.

6. Refrigerate and serve cold, seasoning to taste with salt and pepper just before serving.

Tip: After you cut the kernels from an ear of corn, run the back of the knife down the rows, pressing down to milk that rich liquor. It adds a delicious corn essence.

Pasta Pizza

Here's a fun way to do a pasta side dish. The eggs help the pasta stick together like a pizza, and the secret is to run a rolling pin over the mixture just before you bake it to flatten out the pasta and vegetables.

Serves 6 to 8

1 pound ziti, rigatoni, or other medium pasta shape

1 tablespoon olive oil or vegetable oil

1 (8-ounce) can tomato sauce

2 tablespoons minced fresh oregano

2 tablespoons minced fresh parsley

1/4 cup grated Romano cheese

1 teaspoon minced garlic

1/2 teaspoon crushed red pepper flakes (optional)

1 (16-ounce) can crushed tomatoes

2 large eggs, lightly beaten

1 medium green bell pepper, seeded and chopped

1 large sweet onion, such as Maui, Walla Walla, or Vidalia, sliced

1 cup shredded mozzarella cheese (about 4 ounces)

Grated Parmigiano-Reggiano cheese, to serve

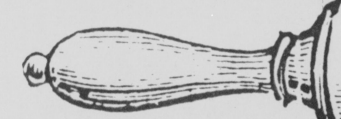

1. Preheat the oven to 400°F. Cook the pasta according to the package directions, reducing the cooking time by 1 to 2 minutes; drain.

2. Spray a deep-dish pizza pan (with a rim) with nonstick cooking spray.

3. In a large bowl, toss the pasta with the tomato sauce, herbs, and Romano cheese. In a medium bowl, mix the garlic and red pepper flakes with the tomatoes and eggs and pour this mixture over the pasta. Pour pasta into the sprayed pizza pan.

4. Layer the remaining ingredients over the pasta, ending with the mozzarella, then press down with a flat plate, or use a rolling pin to lightly flatten and compact the pasta and vegetables.

5. Bake for 15 minutes. Remove from the oven and let cool slightly.

6. Cut the pizza into wedges, sprinkle with Parmigiano-Reggiano cheese, and serve.

Tip: You can also cook this in a 9 x 12-inch glass baking dish that you've sprayed with nonstick cooking spray, but a deep-dish pizza pan is much more fun! Or try cooking this in a 10-inch tube pan, filling the hole in the middle with sautéed mushrooms at the table.

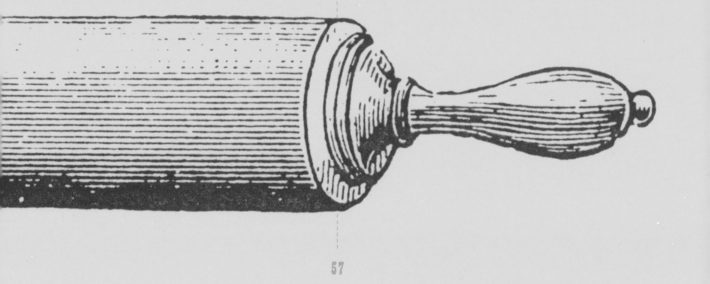

CHAPTER 4 VEGETABLES

There is nothing healthier, more delicious, and more tantalizing than a platter full of buttery garden-fresh sautéed carrots, grilled artichokes, or grilled corn on the cob to add that special dimension to a picnic, barbecue, or family dinner.

Savory French Green Beans

There is nothing as tasty and as fresh —and I mean straight-from-the-garden quality—than crisp green beans. Cooked until they are just tender, the beans in this recipe are further enhanced by the flavors of bacon, garlic, and vinegar. For extra taste, add slivered almonds or cashews, toasted sesame seeds, or snipped chives just before serving.

Serves 4

5 slices bacon, chopped into 1/4-inch pieces

1 pound French green beans

2 tablespoons olive oil

1/3 cup chopped onion

1 1/2 teaspoons minced garlic

1 teaspoon balsamic vinegar

1 teaspoon rice wine vinegar

1 teaspoon dried savory

Salt and pepper

1. In a medium skillet, cook the bacon until crisp. Remove from the pan and drain on paper towels.

2. Cut the beans in half and put them in a steamer to cook until they are just tender.

3. In a large, nonstick skillet, heat the olive oil. Add the onions, garlic, and vinegars, and sauté until limp.

4. Add the bacon, beans, savory, and salt and pepper to taste. Toss the beans to coat evenly, and sauté the mixture until it's warmed through. Serve immediately.

Tip: Fresh green beans can be stored for up to a week in a refrigerator. Wrap them in a paper bag or paper towel and then store in a resealable plastic bag.

Julienned Foiled Veggies

This is a fun, rainbow-hued dish that's downright healthy and delicious. Of course, you can add other veggies too. How about some tiny new potatoes, green beans, or julienned carrots?

Serves 4

1 tablespoon plus 1 teaspoon unsalted butter, cut into pieces

1/4 cup crumbled feta or blue cheese

1. Have medium-hot coals ready, or preheat a gas grill.

2. Combine the vegetables, basil, lemon zest, and salt and pepper to taste in a large bowl; toss gently to mix well. Divide the mixture in half.

3. Place each half in the center of a 12 x 12-inch piece of heavy-duty aluminum foil that has been sprayed with nonstick grilling spray.

4. Dot the vegetables with the butter and bring the corners of the foil together to form a pyramid; twist to seal.

5. Grill the foil packets for 15 to 20 minutes, or until the vegetables are tender.

6. Open the packets, sprinkle the cheese over the vegetables, and reseal; let sit for 4 minutes. Serve immediately.

Tip: Any vegetable can be adapted to this recipe. Try rutabagas, zucchini, leeks, scallions, carrots, endive, celery, cabbage, and so on.

8 to 10 cherry tomatoes, halved

1 1/2 cups corn kernels, cut from 3 to 4 medium ears

1 medium red bell pepper, seeded and julienned

1/2 medium green bell pepper, seeded and julienned

1 large onion, sliced

1 tablespoon chopped fresh basil

1/2 teaspoon grated lemon zest

Salt and pepper

Old-Fashioned Cauliflower Pie

Cauliflower is the "plain Jane" of vegetables, but cooked just right, so there still is some crunch in the florets, it's a wonderful vegetable loaded with vitamins. This recipe does it justice in a rich pie of herbs, onions, and cheeses. Don't cook cauliflower in aluminum or iron pots. Aluminum will turn the vegetable yellow, and iron will turn it brown or blue-green.

Serves 6 to 8

Potato crust:

2 cups firmly packed grated potatoes

1/2 teaspoon salt

2 large eggs, beaten

1/4 cup grated onion

2 scallions, thinly sliced

Vegetable oil

Filling:

1/2 teaspoon salt

3 large eggs, beaten

1/4 cup half-and-half

Black pepper

1/4 teaspoon paprika

3 tablespoons butter

1/2 cup chopped onion

4 scallions, chopped

1/2 teaspoon minced garlic

1/2 teaspoon seasoned salt

1 teaspoon dried savory

1/2 teaspoon dried thyme

1/2 teaspoon dried oregano

2 tablespoons chopped fresh parsley leaves

1 large head cauliflower, broken into small florets

1 cup shredded Cheddar cheese (about 4 ounces)

1 cup shredded Swiss cheese (about 4 ounces)

Paprika, to serve

1. Preheat the oven to 400°F. Spray a 9-inch pie pan with nonstick cooking spray.

2. To make the potato crust, place the grated potato in a colander. Add the salt to the potatoes and let them sit for 10 minutes. Then, using paper towels, squeeze out the excess water.

3. In a medium bowl, combine the potatoes, eggs, onion, and scallions and stir to mix well. Pat the mixture into the pie pan, building up the sides of the crust with lightly floured fingers.

4. Bake for 35 to 40 minutes, or until golden brown. After the first 20 minutes, brush the crust with vegetable oil to help it brown.

5. Remove from the oven and let cool slightly. Reduce the oven temperature to 350°F.

6. While the potato crust is baking, beat together the salt, eggs, half-and-half, pepper to taste, and paprika in a small bowl; set aside.

7. Melt the butter in a large pan over medium heat. Sauté the onions, scallions, garlic, and seasoned salt until the onions soften and the garlic just begins to color. Add the savory, thyme, oregano, parsley, and cauliflower and cook, covered, for 10 minutes, stirring occasionally. Remove from the heat.

8. Layer the baked potato crust with half of the cheeses, then the cauliflower-herb mixture, then the remaining cheese. Pour the half-and-half mixture over the top.

9. Bake for 35 to 40 minutes, until the filling is firm and set and the top is just beginning to brown. Remove from the oven, let sit for 10 minutes, sprinkle with paprika, and serve.

Tip: You can also make this dish with a commercially prepared frozen pie shell, but the extra work will pay off if you make the potato crust.

Three Corns in the Fountain (er, Barbecue)

"Three corns in the fountain, each one bringing happiness." With apologies to the Four Aces, here are three different and delicious ways of cooking corn on the cob on a barbecue grill. There may be small differences in the corn's color, flavor, and tenderness with each cooking method, but each should provide a delicious way to eat America's favorite outdoor veggie. All varieties of corn are great barbecued, but my personal favorite is Peaches & Cream (also called Butter & Sugar), which is also outstanding when boiled or steamed.

Serves 4

Butter spread:

1/2 cup (1 stick) butter, softened

1/2 teaspoon celery salt

5 or 6 grinds of black pepper

Butter-mayo spread:

2 tablespoons mayonnaise

1 tablespoon lemon juice

2 tablespoons butter, softened

1 teaspoon chili powder

1/2 teaspoon salt

1/2 teaspoon garlic powder

4 medium ears white or yellow sweet corn with husks

To make the spreads, mix the ingredients together in separate small bowls, and let them sit at room temperature while cooking the corn.

Method 1:

1. Take the ears of corn, with husks and silks, and put them in a bucket of warm water to which you've added 1 cup sugar and 1 cup milk; soak for 4 hours. Briefly drain and wipe off the husks when ready to cook.

2. Place the corn on a grill over medium-high heat and cook, turning often, for 12 to 14 minutes.

3. When the corn is done, peel off the husks, pull off the silks (much easier than when they were raw), and serve with the spreads on the side.

Method 2:

1. Peel the husks down off the corn, leaving them attached, then carefully remove the silk. Spread one of the butter spreads on the corn, then reposition the husks and tie them at the top with string.

2. Place the corn on the grill over medium-high heat and cook for 12 to 14 minutes, turning every 2 to 3 minutes, making sure that the butter drippings don't flare up and burn the corn.

3. When the corn is done, remove it from the grill, cut the string, peel down the husks, and retie them (with new string) to use as a handle to hold the corn. Eat as is, with no additional butter or spread needed.

Method 3:

1. Leaving the husks and silk intact, just rinse the corn under cold water and shake off the water.

2. Place the corn on the grill over high heat, turning the ears as each section of outside husks blackens and chars, until all the sides are black and charred, about 15 minutes.

3. When the corn is done, remove the husks and silk and serve with the spreads on the side.

Tip: Fully ripe sweet corn has bright green, moist husks. The silk is stiff, dark, and moist, and you should be able to feel the individual kernels by pressing gently against the husk. Fresh corn should be cooked and served the day it is picked or purchased, if possible.

Grilled Cabbage

Cabbage is often overlooked when people think of barbecue side dishes, but it is a delicious and nutritious vegetable that adds a nice flavor, and tons of vitamins, to any meal. My mother, Dorothy Browne, learned to make this during the Depression. She still served it to us in the 1960s, and it was just as delicious.

Serves 4

1 large head green cabbage, quartered and cored

1 slice bacon, chopped

1 small onion, chopped

1/4 cup (1/2 stick) butter, cut into pieces

Salt and pepper

1. Have coals ready for grilling over indirect heat, or preheat a gas grill to low. Spray the inside of a large aluminum cooking bag with nonstick cooking spray.

2. Lay the cabbage, bacon, onions, and butter in the cooking bag, and add salt and pepper to taste.

3. Seal the bag and place on the grill. If using charcoal, place the cooking bag away from the direct heat of the coals.

4. Turn the bag over periodically to avoid burning.

5. The cabbage is done when soft, about 20 minutes for gas, 25 to 30 minutes over charcoal.

Tip: Instead of normal salt, try celery salt or garlic salt for extra flavor.

Blue-Baked Tomatoes

Maytag blue cheese, America's most famous blue cheese, was created by Fritz Maytag, son of the founder of the appliance company, working in conjunction with Iowa State University. Maybe he was waiting for a repair call and had nothing else to do. This is a wonderful savory dish for a summer picnic or barbecue dinner. The zesty cheese, tangy cumin, and luscious tomatoes make for a fine salad or side dish.

Serves 4

4 medium tomatoes, peeled

1 cup thick blue cheese salad dressing

1/2 teaspoon ground cumin

1/4 cup sliced scallion

4 slices crisp bacon, crumbled

2 tablespoons crumbled blue cheese

4 teaspoons snipped chives

1. Preheat the broiler to high heat.

2. Slice the stem end from the tomatoes. Make 3 or 4 vertical cuts into the top of each tomato, cutting about halfway through. Place the tomatoes, cut side up, in an ungreased 8-inch square baking dish. Pour 1/4 inch of water into the baking dish.

3. In a small bowl, combine the dressing, cumin, and scallions. Spoon a heaping tablespoon over each tomato.

4. Broil for 4 minutes, or until the dressing is bubbly and lightly browned.

5. Remove the tomatoes from the oven and garnish with the crumbled bacon, blue cheese, and chives. Serve hot.

Tip: If you don't like blue cheese, try asiago, feta, or even a nice, rich Brie.

Grilled Marinated Portobello Mushrooms

Did you know that cremini mushrooms are really baby portobellos? Besides tasting good, mushrooms are loaded with protein, B vitamins, and minerals, and they are also low in calories. Not bad for a fungus! Don't overcook the mushrooms in this recipe, as we want them still firm and only slightly soft around the edges. The rich earthy flavors mix well with the onion, garlic, and rosemary.

Serves 4

4 large portobello mushroom caps

3 cups dry red wine

2 tablespoons minced shallot or red onion

2 tablespoons chopped garlic

1/4 cup olive oil

1 tablespoon chopped fresh rosemary leaves

1/2 teaspoon dried thyme

Salt and pepper

1. Place the mushrooms in a shallow pan. Combine the remaining ingredients, including salt and pepper to taste, in a small bowl and pour over the mushrooms. Marinate for 1 to 2 hours, turning several times.

2. Have hot coals ready, or preheat a gas grill. Remove the mushrooms from the marinade and grill for 3 minutes on each side.

3. Slice and serve as a side dish or main course.

Tip: Champignons blonde mushrooms, depending on their size, are known as cremini mushrooms when small and portobellos when large.

Grilled 'Chokes

According to Miss Piggy, "[Artichokes] are just plain annoying. After all the trouble you go to, you get about as much actual 'food' out of eating an artichoke as you would from licking 30 or 40 postage stamps. Have the shrimp cocktail instead." She obviously never had these slightly sweet and tangy, marinated and grilled artichokes.

Serves 8

4 large artichokes (with the longest stems you can find)

1/4 cup balsamic vinegar

1/4 cup water

1 tablespoon brown sugar

1/4 cup soy sauce

1 tablespoon minced ginger

1/4 cup olive oil

1. Slice the artichoke tops off crosswise and, using a vegetable peeler, pare the stems until you reach a light green interior.

2. Boil or steam the artichokes in a large pot with 2 to 3 inches of water until the bottoms pierce easily or a petal pulls off easily, about 20 minutes. Drain the artichokes and let cool to room temperature.

3. Cut each artichoke in half lengthwise and scrape out the fuzzy center and any purple-tipped petals.

4. Mix the remaining ingredients in a large plastic bag and add the artichokes to the bag, turning them over several times to coat all sides. For the best flavor, marinate in the mixture overnight in the refrigerator; if you are in a hurry, marinate for at least 2 hours.

5. Have medium-hot coals ready, or preheat a gas grill to medium. Drain the artichokes and place, cut side down, on the grill. Grill until lightly browned on the cut side, 5 to 7 minutes.

6. Turn the artichokes over and drizzle the remaining marinade over them. Grill until the petal tips are lightly charred, 3 to 4 minutes more. Serve hot or at room temperature

Tip: Make other dishes unique by adding artichoke hearts. Vegetable soups, pasta dishes, and salads all benefit from having artichokes in the mix.

Roasted and Stuffed Red Onions

These onions present beautifully with grilled steaks, roast pork, prime rib roast, or with pork or beef ribs. Serve them alongside garlic mashed potatoes and Yorkshire pudding.

Serves 4

4 large red onions

2 tablespoons butter

3 cloves garlic, finely diced

1 (16-ounce) can corn, drained

1 small red bell pepper, seeded and finely diced

20 medium brown mushrooms (cremini, button, or other favorite)

1/2 teaspoon Worcestershire sauce

1 teaspoon grated lemon zest

1 tablespoon chopped fresh thyme

Sea salt

Cracked black pepper

1. Preheat the oven to 300°F or prepare a grill for cooking over indirect heat. Roast the red onions until tender, about 30 minutes. The time will vary depending on the size of the onion. Remove from the oven and let cool.

2. Remove the outside layer of the onions and discard, then cut off and discard the top third. Using a melon baller or grapefruit spoon, scoop out the center of the onions to form cups.

3. Chop the onions that you scooped out. Melt 1 tablespoon of butter in a medium skillet and sauté the chopped onions with the diced garlic, corn, and bell pepper for 5 minutes.

4. Cut the mushrooms into quarters and add to the onion-corn mixture. Cook until tender and juicy.

5. Add the Worcestershire sauce and lemon zest and cook until most of the moisture has evaporated. Add the thyme and season well with sea salt and cracked black pepper to taste.

6. Spoon the warm mixture into the onion cups until slightly overfilled. Melt the remaining tablespoon of butter and brush over the tops of the onions.

7. Warm in the oven and serve immediately.

Tip: You can use sweet onions, such as Maui, Walla Walla, or Vidalia, instead of red ones and substitute frozen peas for the corn if you wish.

Grilled Belgian Endive

Belgian endive is a delightful vegetable that goes well with roasts and roasted chicken. The delicate flavor, sometimes a bit bitter, can be enhanced with citrus juices and vinegar, as it is in this dish.

Serves 4

1 large navel orange

1 tablespoon rice wine vinegar

4 tablespoons olive oil

Garlic salt

Black pepper

4 medium Belgian endives

1. With a vegetable peeler, remove the zest from the orange and cut it lengthwise into very thin strips.

2. Squeeze enough juice from the orange to measure 2 tablespoons.

3. In a bowl, whisk together the orange zest, orange juice, vinegar, 2 tablespoons of oil, and garlic salt and pepper to taste until well mixed.

4. Have medium-hot coals ready, or preheat a gas grill to 300°F.

5. Halve the endives lengthwise, keeping the halves from separating into leaves, and brush them all over with the remaining 2 tablespoons oil.

6. Season the endives to taste with salt and pepper and grill, cut side down, on a well-seasoned grill rack until the edges start to brown, about 3 minutes. Serve drizzled with the orange vinaigrette.

Tip: Select smooth and white endives with yellow tips and leaves that are closed at the tips. Slice off about 1/8 inch from the stem end. Then cut a cone shape about 1/2 inch deep from the stem end.

Classic

Cabbage Casserole

This side dish's flavorings of cabbage, smoky bacon, onion, cream, and cheese are very complimentary for just about any meat or fish main course. And cabbage is rich in vitamin C (an antioxidant) and fiber and is also a member of the cruciferous vegetable family, which may help reduce the risk of several kinds of cancer.

Serves 4 to 6

1/2 pound bacon, chopped (optional)

4 cups (3 cups green, 1 cup red) shredded cabbage (about one pound)

1 teaspoon salt

2 tablespoons all-purpose flour

1/8 teaspoon white pepper

1 large onion, finely chopped

3 tablespoons butter, cut into pieces

2 cups milk or half-and-half

1 cup shredded Swiss or Emmental cheese

1. Preheat the oven to 375°F. If using, cook the bacon in a medium skillet over medium heat until crisp. Drain, chop, and set aside.
2. Spread half of the cabbage in a buttered 9 x 13-inch pan. Combine the salt, flour, and pepper, and sprinkle half of this mixture over the cabbage.
3. Sprinkle half of the onion and half of the bacon over the cabbage.
4. Repeat the layers of cabbage, flour mixture, onion, and bacon. Dot the top with the butter. Pour the milk over the top, completely covering the mixture.
5. Cover the pan and bake for 30 minutes.
6. Uncover and sprinkle the cheese over the top, then bake for 15 minutes longer. Serve hot.

Tip: You may wish to add 1 tablespoon of caraway seeds or poppy seeds to the cheese topping before serving.

Bourbon Creamed Corn

A super picnic or holiday side dish, this creamy corn is festive and quite tasty. It's superb with roast beef or roast leg of lamb, but is also great by itself over thickly buttered slices of homemade bread that you've toasted and rubbed with a raw garlic clove.

Serves 6 to 8

1/4 cup butter

1 cup chopped shallots (3 to 4 large)

1 1/2 teaspoons minced garlic

1 large red bell pepper, seeded and finely chopped

3 cups corn kernels, cut from 4 to 5 medium ears

2/3 cup heavy cream

1/4 cup bourbon

1 1/4 cups chopped scallion

Salt and pepper

Paprika, to serve

1. Melt the butter in a large, heavy skillet over medium-high heat. Add the shallots and garlic and sauté for 2 minutes.

2. Add the bell pepper and sauté for 1 minute.

3. Add the corn kernels and sauté until almost tender, about 2 minutes.

4. Add 1/3 cup of cream and the bourbon and simmer the sauce, stirring often, until it thickly coats the corn, about 2 minutes.

5. Add the remaining 1/3 cup cream and 1 cup of scallions, and simmer the mixture until the sauce thickens enough to coat the corn kernels, about 2 minutes longer.

6. Season the creamed corn to taste with salt and pepper, then transfer to a serving bowl and sprinkle with the remaining 1/4 cup scallions. Sprinkle with paprika for color, and serve.

Tip: You can substitute whiskey, rum, or brandy for the bourbon.

Olde Thyme Corn Pudding

One of the dishes shared with the Pilgrims at Plymouth Rock was a creamed corn dish prepared by the Indians. This is a slightly more modern version with a bit more flavor and fresher taste.

Serves 4 to 6

1 (16-ounce) can corn

1 (16-ounce) can cream-style corn

1/2 cup yellow cornmeal

1 tablespoon minced fresh thyme

1/4 cup chopped onion

1/4 cup finely diced red bell pepper

1/4 cup (1/2 stick) butter

2 large eggs, beaten

1 cup milk or half-and-half

Salt and pepper

1. Preheat the oven to 350°F.
2. In a medium bowl, mix together all the ingredients, including salt and pepper to taste, and put in a buttered 2-quart casserole.
3. Bake for about 40 minutes. The pudding should be lightly brown and firm in the middle. Serve hot.

Tip: Fresh corn, if you have it, tastes much better in this pudding. Just slice the kernels from 4 ears and use instead of the 16-ounce can corn.

Green Bean Bake

This comfort dish has perhaps been seen on more Thanksgiving and Christmas dinner tables than any other dish except turkey and cranberry sauce. But it's still a crowd pleaser at any dinner.

Serves 6

1 (10 1/2-ounce) can cream of mushroom soup

1/2 cup milk or half-and-half

1 teaspoon soy sauce

1/4 teaspoon black pepper

2 (9-ounce) packages frozen cut green beans, cooked and drained

1 large sweet onion, such as Maui, Walla Walla, or Vidalia, finely chopped

1 (2.8-ounce) can French-fried onions

1. Preheat the oven to 350°F.
2. In a 1 1/2-quart casserole, combine the soup, milk, soy sauce, and pepper.
3. Add the beans and chopped onions, and stir.
4. Bake for 25 minutes, or until the dish is hot and bubbling; stir. Top with the French-fried onions and bake for 5 minutes more. Serve hot.

Tip: Substitute the same amount of fresh or frozen broccoli and cream of broccoli soup and you have another favorite American side dish.

Classic
Country Fried Corn

Fried corn is a staple in the Amish country of Pennsylvania. Steaming bowls are served up at lunch and dinner, and the nutty sweet corn adds a wonderful flavor to roast beef or pork tenderloin.

Serves 4 to 8

4 thick slices bacon

1/2 small onion, chopped

8 medium ears sweet corn, with husks removed

Salt and pepper

1. In a large skillet, fry the bacon over medium heat until crisp. Place the slices on paper towels to drain and pour off all but 2 tablespoons of fat from the pan. Chop the bacon into 1/4-inch pieces and set aside.
2. Add the onions to the fat in the skillet and sauté over medium heat until soft.
3. Cut the kernels from the ears, and scrape the ears with the back of your knife to get all the corn milk.
4. Add the corn and corn milk to the onions in the skillet and cook for 2 to 3 minutes. Then add the bacon, season to taste with salt and pepper, and serve.

Tip: Keep fresh corn in the refrigerator once you bring it home from the farmers market or grocery store. Fresh corn on the cob will lose up to 40 percent of its sugar content after 6 hours of room temperature storage. The sugar is converted to starch.

Crispy Fried Okra

A classic Southern dish, fresh okra, fried just right, is tender, full of flavor, and loaded with vitamins. Serve with a shaker of Parmesan cheese for people to sprinkle on just before eating. A bowl of ranch dressing is also nice for dipping.

Serves 4

Oil, for frying

1 pound okra

2 large eggs, beaten

4 to 6 dashes hot pepper sauce, such as Tabasco

1/2 cup yellow cornmeal

1/2 cup white cornmeal

1/2 teaspoon salt

1 teaspoon sugar

1/2 teaspoon cayenne pepper

1. Heat 3 inches of oil in a Dutch oven or deep cast iron pot to 375°F.

2. Wash the okra, cutting off both ends, and drain well in a colander. Cut into 3-inch lengths, and then quarter each piece lengthwise so you have 4 spears.

3. In a large bowl, combine the beaten eggs and hot sauce. Add the okra and stir to coat each spear well.

4. In a shallow dish, combine the yellow and white cornmeal, salt, sugar, and cayenne pepper.

5. Dip the okra pieces into the cornmeal mixture to coat each spear well.

6. Fry the okra in the oil, in batches, until nicely browned, 4 to 6 minutes for each batch.

7. Drain on paper towels and serve immediately.

Tip: When shopping, look for tender okra pods that are under 4 1/2 inches long, with tips that bend under slight pressure. Fresh okra should be bright green and free from blemishes.

Classic
Fried Green Tomatoes

These are a delicious accompaniment to fried chicken, thick slices of ham, or grilled fish. In the 1800s, tomato fritters, sliced tomatoes rolled in flour and cornmeal, were popular, and they evolved into this tasty side dish, using firmer green tomatoes.

Serves 2 to 4

1 large egg

1/4 cup buttermilk

3 or 4 drops Louisiana hot sauce

1/4 cup yellow cornmeal

1/4 teaspoon granulated garlic

Salt and pepper

3 medium green tomatoes, sliced 1/4 inch thick

1 tablespoon olive oil and 1 tablespoon bacon drippings (from 2 to 3 slices bacon), mixed

1. In a shallow bowl, whisk the egg, buttermilk, and hot sauce until well mixed.

2. Spread the cornmeal on a plate and add the garlic and salt and pepper to taste. Stir well to incorporate.

3. Dip the tomato slices in the egg mixture, then coat both sides with the cornmeal. Set aside on a separate plate.

4. In a large cast iron skillet, heat 1 tablespoon of oil-dripping mixture over moderate heat and slide in about half of the tomato slices, without crowding. Cook for 2 minutes on each side, or until the tomatoes are golden brown.

5. Transfer the slices to paper towels to drain and repeat with the remaining tomatoes and oil mixture. Serve immediately, as they lose their crispy texture upon standing.

Tip: Serve these with salsa, sour cream, or corn relish for a different taste.

Glazed Carrots

Loaded with vitamins, carrots have long been a staple of American meals. Don't over-cook them—they should still resist a fork. Serve this sweet and lightly spiced dish with just about any meat, fish, or poultry.

Serves 6

6 large carrots, peeled

12 small white onions, peeled

3 tablespoons butter

1 tablespoon sugar

1/3 cup light molasses

1/4 teaspoon salt

1/4 teaspoon ground ginger

1/4 teaspoon ground allspice

1/4 teaspoon grated lemon zest

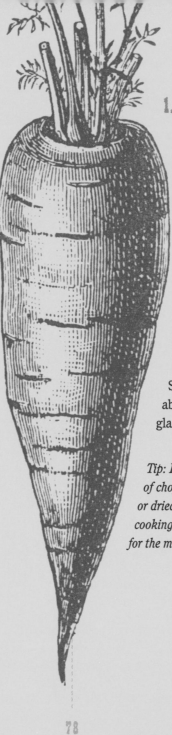

1. In separate medium saucepans, boil the carrots and onions in enough salted water to cover for 20 minutes, or just until crisp-tender; drain well.

2. Melt the butter in a large skillet and stir in the sugar, molasses, salt, spices, and lemon zest.

3. Heat, stirring constantly, to the boiling point. Add the carrots and onions, stirring to coat well with the syrup. Simmer, stirring frequently, for about 10 minutes, or until nicely glazed. Serve hot.

Tip: For a lively touch, add a cup of chopped apricots, golden raisins, or dried cherries to the mixture while cooking. You can also substitute honey for the molasses.

Acorn Squash with Maple Syrup

A touch of butter and maple syrup is all it takes to turn this dish into a nutty-sweet masterpiece of golden color and natural sweetness. Antioxidants, minerals, and true fall taste—this acorn squash has it all.

Serves 4

2 small to medium acorn squash

3 tablespoons unsalted butter, softened

1/2 teaspoon kosher salt

Ground black pepper

4 tablespoons maple syrup

1 teaspoon ground nutmeg

1 teaspoon ground cinnamon

1. Preheat the oven to 400°F.

2. Cut the squash in half lengthwise, perpendicular to the ribs, and scoop out the seeds.

3. Spray a 9 x 12-inch glass baking dish with nonstick cooking spray and pour in 1/4 inch of water.

4. Set the squash halves, cut side up, in the prepared baking pan and smear the flesh with the softened butter. Sprinkle the flesh with salt and pepper.

5. Drizzle a tablespoon of maple syrup over the cut edge and into the hollow of each squash half, then sprinkle the flesh with the nutmeg and cinnamon.

6. Roast the squash halves until nicely browned and very tender when pierced with a fork, about 1 hour and 15 minutes. Do not undercook. Serve warm.

Tip: Instead of maple syrup, you can use maple sugar, brown sugar, or turbinado sugar. Sprinkle 1 tablespoon of sugar over each squash half.

99 LBS. NET WEIGHT

WHOLE BEAN
UNCOATED

CHAPTER 5 **RICE**

TABLE RICE

There's a reason that the Chinese often greet visitors by saying, "Have you had rice today?" These small, friendly grains are a comfort food that goes with just about any entrée and can be featured in dozens of mouth-watering, quickly prepared dishes.

Wild Mushroom Risotto

Risotto is simply rice, usually arborio, sautéed in butter then cooked and stirred as stock or other liquid is slowly added in small amounts. As each addition of stock is absorbed by the grains, another is added until the rice is creamy and tender. Like this recipe, you can add herbs, mushrooms, onions, garlic, cheese, or all of the above for some extra flavor.

Serves 6

5 cups duck or chicken stock

1 cup dried porcini mushrooms

6 tablespoons unsalted butter

1 tablespoon olive oil

1/2 cup finely minced onion

Pinch of granulated garlic

Pinch of dried savory

1/2 cup sliced shiitake mushrooms

1/2 cup sliced chanterelle mushrooms

1/2 cup sliced cremini mushrooms

2 cups arborio rice

3/4 cup port wine

Salt and pepper

2 cups grated Parmigiano-Reggiano cheese (about 6 ounces)

1. In a medium saucepan, heat the stock and the dried porcini mushrooms to a simmer and keep warm until ready to use.

2. Heat the butter and oil over medium heat in a medium, heavy saucepan. When the butter is melted, add the onions and cook until translucent, about 5 minutes, stirring occasionally.

3. Add the garlic, savory, and mushrooms and sauté for about 2 minutes, stirring constantly.

4. Add the rice and cook, stirring constantly, until the rice is coated with butter and oil and begins to be opaque, about 3 minutes. Reduce the heat to low.

5. Remove the porcini mushrooms from the stock with a slotted spoon, cut off any tough or stringy parts, and coarsely chop.

6. Add the porcini mushrooms and the port to the rice and stir for 1 minute, then add 2 cups of the hot stock, stirring constantly until the liquid is almost completely absorbed. Season to taste with salt and pepper as you stir.

7. Continue adding stock, 1/2 cup at a time, as the liquid is absorbed, stirring constantly. The risotto is ready when it is slightly firm when you bite into a grain. This process takes 20 to 25 minutes.

8. Stir in 1 1/2 cups of Parmesan cheese just before serving. Sprinkle a little of the remaining 1/2 cup on top of each serving. Serve as a side dish with barbecued duck or venison, roast pheasant or quail, grilled ham, or grilled veal chops.

Tip: When adding liquids to risotto, it helps to have them hot when you pour them into the rice. That way they are absorbed more easily and don't slow down the cooking process.

Classic
Lemon Grass and Coconut Rice

I learned how to prepare this dish at a cooking school in Bangkok, Thailand. Go to a local Asian market and get fresh lemon grass if you want the best the recipe can offer. You'll be rewarded with an exotic, flavorful, and easy rice dish that goes well with any Thai, Chinese, Japanese, or other Asian meal. This has been cooked in Thailand for at least 100 years.

Serves 4

1 teaspoon butter

1 cup long-grain white rice

1 cup water

1/2 cup coconut milk

1 tablespoon minced lemon grass

1 teaspoon unsweetened coconut flakes

1. Melt the butter in a medium saucepan that has a snug-fitting lid. Add the rice and stir to coat each grain.

2. Add the water, coconut milk, lemon grass, and coconut flakes. Stir and bring to a boil. Reduce the heat to the lowest setting, and cover.

3. From this point on, do not stir the rice. Cook for 25 minutes and then shut off the heat.

4. Remove the pan from the burner and leave it covered for 20 minutes. Do not stir until the time is up. To serve, put the rice into a serving bowl and take to the table immediately.

Tip: Adding grilled shrimp, scallops, fish, or lobster to this side dish makes it into a delicious main course.

Sticky Rice Cakes

Japanese cookbook author Shizuo Tsuji notes: "Rice is a beautiful food. It is beautiful when it grows, precision rows of sparkling green stalks shooting up to reach the hot summer sun. It is beautiful when harvested, autumn gold sheaves piled on diked, patchwork paddies. It is beautiful when, once threshed, it enters granary bins like a flood of tiny seed-pearls. It is beautiful when cooked by a practiced hand, pure white and sweetly fragrant." This dish is a soft cake of rice and mushrooms that can be eaten as an appetizer, side dish, or light lunch with some grilled fish or poultry.

Serves 4

5 tablespoons butter

1 medium onion, finely diced

2 cups finely diced porcini or cremini mushrooms

1 cup short-grain brown rice

2 cups vegetable stock

4 scallions, cut into 2-inch slivers

1 teaspoon nuoc nam (Asian fish sauce)

1 large egg yolk

2 tablespoons fresh white bread crumbs

1 teaspoon granulated garlic

1/4 cup chopped fresh parsley

Salt and pepper

1. Melt 3 tablespoons of butter in a large saucepan over medium heat, then add the onions and mushrooms and cook for about 5 minutes, until the onions are softened and translucent.

2. Add the rice and cook, stirring, for 1 to 2 minutes, until each grain is well coated with the butter. Add the vegetable stock and stir to make sure the rice is mixed in.

3. Cover the pan and reduce the heat to maintain a simmer. Cook for 25 to 30 minutes, until all the liquid is absorbed and the rice is sticky.

4. Stir in the scallions, nuoc nam, egg yolk, bread crumbs, garlic, and parsley, and season to taste with salt and pepper.

5. Scoop the rice mixture into a shallow dish, cover it with parchment or wax paper, and let the rice cool to room temperature. Refrigerate for 2 to 3 hours, until very cold. In 1/4-cup handfuls, shape the rice into 6 patties and place on a tray lined with wax paper (or aluminum foil).

6. Cover and refrigerate the cakes until you are ready to cook them.

7. Heat the remaining 2 tablespoons butter in a large skillet, or melt the butter on your barbecue griddle. Add the rice cakes, cooking for approximately 2 minutes on each side, turning them carefully with a spatula, until golden brown on both sides.

8. Serve as a side dish with grilled shrimp or fish, pork chops and cutlets, or roasted chicken or game hens.

Tip: Instead of individual rice cakes, make one large cake. Brown in a large nonstick skillet, and serve covered with grilled shrimp, stir-fried vegetables, or seared scallops.

Curried Rice and Lentil Loaf

Lentils are one of the forgotten grains, but dishes like this bring out their rich, nutty flavor. It is a hearty, nutritious, nonfat recipe, which includes rich brown lentils and nutritious wild rice, veggies, garlic, pecans (or peanuts), and a healthy touch of curry. Serve alongside roast duck, venison steaks, or thick slices of country ham.

Serves 4

1 1/2 cups vegetable stock

3 tablespoons soy sauce

3/4 cup brown lentils, rinsed and debris removed

1 cup cooked wild rice

1/2 cup oat bran

1/2 cup finely chopped celery

1/2 cup finely chopped carrots

1/2 cup finely chopped mushrooms, both stems and caps

1/4 cup finely chopped onion

1/2 cup chopped pecans, or other favorite nut

1 1/2 to 2 teaspoons minced garlic

2 teaspoons curry powder

1/2 teaspoon dried savory

1/2 teaspoon dried sage

1/2 teaspoon black pepper

1. Preheat the oven or a grill to 375°F.

2. Bring the vegetable stock to a boil in a medium saucepan, then add 1 tablespoon of soy sauce and the lentils. Reduce the heat to low and simmer for 30 minutes, or until the lentils are tender. Do not drain.

3. In a large bowl, combine the lentil mixture, wild rice, bran, celery, carrots, mushrooms, onions, pecans, garlic, curry, savory, sage, and pepper, stirring vigorously to help break down the lentils.

4. Pack the mixture firmly into a well-greased 5 x 9-inch loaf pan. Brush the top of the loaf with the remaining 2 tablespoons soy sauce, and bake for 45 to 50 minutes, or until crisp on the outside.

5. Let stand for 10 minutes before slicing and serving.

Tip: For a firmer loaf, add 2 large beaten eggs to the lentil mixture before you pack it into the loaf pan. You can also add peeled, chopped hard-boiled eggs for a bit more protein.

Saffron-Golden Raisin Rice

Saffron filaments, or threads, are actually the dried stigmas of the saffron flower. Each flower contains only three stigmas, which must be picked by hand, and it takes more than 75,000 flowers to produce just 1 pound of saffron filaments. It is the world's most precious spice. The lively yellow color and heavenly scent of this rice goes well with the juicy raisins to brighten up your plate.

Serves 4

4 cups chicken or vegetable stock

3/4 teaspoon saffron powder

1/2 teaspoon ground cardamom

Salt and pepper

1 tablespoon olive oil or butter

1/2 teaspoon minced garlic

2 cups long-grain rice, such as basmati or Texmati

2 cups golden raisins, soaked in warm water for 20 minutes

1. Bring the chicken stock to a boil in a large saucepan.

2. Put the saffron and cardamom in a small bowl and add 1 tablespoon of the hot stock. Mix until dissolved, then pour back into the boiling stock.

3. Add salt and pepper to taste, the oil, garlic, and rice. Stir once, then cover the pot tightly, letting the rice cook over low heat for about 25 minutes. Please resist the urge to open the lid.

4. When the rice is cooked, the grains will remain separate and free of clumps when fluffed with a fork. Remove the pot from the heat, drain the rice, and add the drained raisins. Stir well and let sit for 4 minutes. Fluff with a fork again and serve.

Tip: For an extra bit of color and flavor, instead of raisins use 1 cup dried cherries and 1 cup dried apricots, both cut into raisin-sized chunks, soaked in warm water for 20 minutes, and drained.

Mexican Green Rice

Visually intriguing, tasty, and a bit different from the usual Mexican red rice, this side dish is perfect with chicken or pork. It is guaranteed to jazz up even the simplest grilled meat or vegetable meal. Avocado slices make a nice garnish.

Serves 4

1 cup long-grain white rice

2 tablespoons vegetable oil

3 small or 2 large poblano chile peppers, roasted, seeded, and peeled

1/2 medium onion, chopped

2 cloves garlic, chopped

2 to 3 sprigs fresh parsley

2 to 3 sprigs fresh cilantro

2 1/2 cups chicken or vegetable stock

1/2 cup fresh or thawed frozen peas (optional)

Salt

1. In a medium bowl, soak the rice in enough hot water to cover for 15 minutes, then rinse in a strainer under running water until the water runs clear.

2. Drain and let dry.

3. Heat the oil in a medium saucepan over medium heat and sauté the rice, stirring to prevent sticking or burning, until golden, 10 to 15 minutes. Set aside.

4. Purée the chile peppers, onion, garlic, and herbs in a blender with 1/2 cup of stock.

5. Add the purée to the saucepan. When it has been absorbed by the rice, add the remaining 2 cups stock.

6. Return the saucepan to the stove, cover, and simmer over low heat until all the liquid has been absorbed.

7. Remove from the heat, and add the peas, if using. Stir to fluff, season to taste with salt, and serve immediately.

Tip: This is also great stuffed inside whole red, green, or yellow bell peppers and roasted in the oven. Just steam the bell peppers for 10 minutes, then fill them and cook in a 350°F oven for 20 minutes.

Spanish Rice

The spicy tomato and chicken base of this recipe makes a fine dish to serve with roast or barbecued chicken; grilled or baked fish; Mexican dishes such as pork adobo or carne asada; or charred steaks. Is *mucho bueno* with a chilled margarita, *si?*

Serves 4

1 cup long-grain white rice

3 tablespoons olive oil

1 medium onion, diced small

1/2 teaspoon minced garlic

1 1/2 teaspoons salt

1/4 teaspoon chili powder

1 (10-ounce) can tomato sauce

2 1/4 cups chicken stock

1/4 cup chopped canned chipotle chile peppers in adobo sauce (optional)

1 1/2 cups shredded Monterey Jack cheese (about 6 ounces)

1. In a large skillet, brown the rice in the olive oil over medium heat.

2. When browned, add the onion, garlic, salt, chili powder, tomato sauce, and chicken stock, and let simmer, covered, over low heat for 25 minutes, or until tender. Add the chile peppers, if desired.

3. Transfer the rice to an 8 x 8-inch casserole dish and top with the cheese. Just before serving, melt the cheese under a broiler or in a microwave oven.

Tip: I like to soak the rice in chicken stock for an hour before cooking it in the saucepan, to give it a bit more body and fullness.

Rice with Squash and Pineapple

This spiced, sweet dish is almost a meal in itself, but it serves well alongside grilled pork chops. Most winter squash has an extended shelf life and can be kept for up to 3 months in a cool, dry place (between 55° and 60°F). Do not store acorn or other squash in the refrigerator or they will spoil much more quickly.

Serves 4 to 6

1 large acorn squash

2 cups chicken stock

1/2 cup long-grain white rice

1/2 cup wild rice

1 cup diced carrots

1 cup diced onions

1 cup canned crushed pineapple (about 10 ounces)

1/2 cup dried cherries

2 tablespoons orange juice concentrate

3 tablespoons dark molasses

1 tablespoon packed brown sugar

1/2 teaspoon ground cinnamon

1/4 teaspoon ground allspice

1/4 teaspoon ground nutmeg

1. Poke the squash several times with a knife and microwave on high power for 10 minutes, or until tender. Let cool.

2. Cut the squash in half lengthwise, remove the seeds and stringy center, then scoop out and coarsely chop the cooked flesh.

3. Meanwhile, in a saucepan over medium-high heat, combine the stock, white rice, and wild rice and bring to a boil.

4. Reduce the heat to medium-low, cover, cook for 20 minutes, then add the onions and carrots. Cover and cook for an additional 10 minutes, or until the rice, onions, and carrots are tender and most of the liquid has been absorbed. The wild rice will still be a bit firm and undercooked.

5. Add the squash, pineapple, cherries, orange juice concentrate, molasses, sugar, cinnamon, allspice, and nutmeg and cook, uncovered, for 5 minutes more, stirring often, until the rice is heated through. Serve hot.

Tip: As an alternative, use spaghetti squash or pumpkin. Small sugar pumpkins work best if you opt for the latter.

Easy Baked Risotto

Normally, one has to make risotto by standing over a hot stove for up to an hour, constantly stirring, but not here. This is a classic Italian way of making risotto in the oven. It has the same delicious smooth texture and flavor, but requires a lot less elbow grease over a hot burner.

Serves 4 to 6

2 tablespoons butter

4 cups chopped wild mushrooms, such as shiitake, porcini, oyster, or chanterelle

1/4 teaspoon salt

1/4 teaspoon black pepper

1/2 cup finely chopped onions

1 teaspoon minced garlic

1/2 teaspoon dried savory

1 1/2 cups short-grain white rice, such as arborio

1/2 cup dry white wine

3 cups chicken stock

1/2 cup freshly grated Parmesan cheese

1/3 cup coarsely chopped fresh parsley

Shavings Parmesan cheese, to serve

1. Preheat the oven to 350°F.

2. In a large, heavy, ovenproof saucepan, melt the butter over medium-high heat, then add the mushrooms, salt, pepper, onions, garlic, and savory. Cook until the mushrooms are golden and the onions are tender, 5 to 7 minutes.

3. Stir in the rice until well coated, then add the wine and stock and bring to a boil.

4. Transfer the pan to the preheated oven, and bake, stirring occasionally, until all the liquid has been absorbed and the rice is tender but still firm in the center, about 30 minutes.

5. Remove the pan from the oven, stir in the Parmesan cheese and parsley, and serve garnished with shaved Parmesan.

Tip: There are lots of Parmesan cheeses available on the market, but there is only one that makes your heart sing. Parmigiano-Reggiano is the king of cheeses, with a sweet and fruity aroma, like pineapple, and a flavor that is piquant, nutty, and unlike any other cheese in the world.

Seven-Veggie Fried Rice

Here is a nutritious, healthy, and, oh yes, tasty side dish that can double as a main dish for lunch. A harvested rice kernel contains a bran layer and is enclosed by a hull. White rice has had both the bran and hull removed during the milling process. By contrast, brown rice has had only the hull removed. The result is a much more nutritious dish, containing protein and several minerals.

Serves 4 to 6

3 large eggs

1/4 teaspoon salt

1/8 teaspoon black pepper

5 tablespoons oil, or more as needed

1 medium onion, diced

1 large carrot, diced

4 scallions, thinly sliced

Kernels cut from 2 medium ears corn

1/2 cup frozen peas

1 medium red bell pepper, finely diced

1/2 cup shredded Napa cabbage

4 cups cold cooked rice

2 tablespoons oyster sauce, plus more to taste

2 tablespoons dark soy sauce

Salt

Light soy sauce

1. In a small bowl, lightly beat the eggs, adding the salt and pepper.

2. Heat a wok or large, nonstick frying pan over medium-high heat. Add 1 tablespoon of oil, and when hot, pour half of the egg mixture into the wok and cook, turning over once. Remove the egg from the pan to a cutting board.

3. Cook the remaining egg in the same manner, and remove it to the cutting board. Cut all of the eggs into thin strips and then into small squares. Set aside.

4. Add 2 tablespoons of oil to the wok, then add the onions, carrot, scallions, corn, peas, and bell pepper. Stir-fry briefly, then add the cabbage. Continue to stir-fry until the vegetables are cooked to the tenderness desired and they start to turn brown.

5. Add 2 tablespoons of oil, then turn the heat down to medium and add the rice. Use chopsticks to separate the individual grains.

6. Stir in the oyster sauce and dark soy sauce. Season to taste with salt, light soy sauce, or more oyster sauce, if desired. Add the egg and stir well. Serve with a meat, poultry, or fish entrée.

Tip: If you don't have leftover rice, cook up some rice in the morning and then refrigerate it all day to fry up at night. The drier the rice, the more the grains will separate, and the better the fried rice.

Firehouse Rice

Firehouse food has to meet four criteria: it has to taste good, it has to be inexpensive (firefighters pay for their own daily meals), it has to be easy to prepare, and it has to be fairly quick to cook. This recipe is all of the above. There are more than 1.5 million firefighters in the United States, and altogether they are some of the best cooks in the universe. This recipe was given to me by a fire captain from San Diego. It is light yet hearty, and can be stretched to a main course with the addition of grilled chicken, ahi tuna, or barbecued shrimp.

Serves 4 to 6

2 cups long-grain white rice

1 tablespoon salt

1 teaspoon curry powder

2 cups chicken stock

2 cups French onion soup

1 pound button or cremini mushrooms, sliced

1 cup panko (Japanese bread crumbs)

1 cup (2 sticks) butter, sliced into pats

1. Preheat the oven or a grill to 350°F.

2. In a large (14-inch) cast iron frying pan or Dutch oven, combine the rice, salt, and curry powder. Stir and then cover with the chicken stock and onion soup.

3. Sprinkle the mushroom slices and panko over the rice and soup mixture and dot with the pats of butter.

4. Bake in the oven for 1 hour, or until all the liquid has been absorbed by the rice, crumbs, and mushrooms. Serve hot with chicken, fish, pork, or stir-fried vegetables.

Tip: You can substitute any soup for the French onion soup used here. Try tomato, clam chowder, cream of chicken or celery, hearty beef vegetable, or, of course, cream of mushroom. Also, margarine is an acceptable substitute for the 2 sticks of butter, or use a stick of each.

Dirty Rice

No it's not really dirty; it's just that the cooked chicken and some of the spices make the rice look dirty. But man, what a taste. This is rice at its best—full of flavors, spices, textures, and soul. Be careful not to overcook the rice; you want some resistance as you bite into each grain.

Serves 6 to 8

Creole seasoning blend:

2 tablespoons onion powder

2 tablespoons garlic powder

2 tablespoons dried oregano

2 tablespoons dried basil

1 tablespoon dried thyme

1 tablespoon black pepper

1 tablespoon white pepper

1 tablespoon cayenne pepper

5 tablespoons paprika

3 tablespoons salt

4 to 5 pounds chicken livers, gizzards, necks, wings, backs

4 cups water, plus more as needed

1/2 cup (1 stick) butter

2 cups converted rice, such as Uncle Ben's

2 cups chopped onions

1 cup chopped celery

1 cup chopped green or red bell pepper

2 tablespoons minced garlic

1/4 cup chopped fresh parsley

1. To make the Creole seasoning blend, mix together the seasonings and store in an airtight bottle. You will have more than you need for this recipe.

2. Place the chicken parts in the water in a large saucepan with 1 tablespoon of Creole seasoning and boil for about 30 minutes, skimming off any fat that rises to the surface. Cool the chicken, remove the meat from the bones, and discard the bones. Chop the meat into small pieces and return to the liquid in the pot; set aside.

3. In a medium, heavy pot or saucepan, melt the butter and sauté the rice until brown. Add the onions, celery, bell pepper, garlic, and parsley, and sauté until the onions are transparent.

4. Heat the original cooking water containing the deboned chicken pieces and add the rice. The water should cover the chicken and rice by 1 inch. Add more water if necessary.

5. Bring to a boil and cook until the water has almost evaporated. Stir, cover, and cook over low heat for about 25 minutes.

6. Remove from the heat and let stand for about 10 minutes. Stir and serve.

Tip: Instead of boiling the chicken parts, some folks fry them up in a frying pan. Then they chop up the cooked chicken, discarding the bones and cartilage, scrape the browned and burned bits from the pan, and throw them all into that nice white rice—making it even more "dirty."

Rice Pilaf

This is a quick rice pilaf recipe that includes the color of fresh red and green bell peppers. Great with any fowl, such as chicken, duck, turkey, game hens, goose, or quail.

Serves 4

3/4 cup converted rice, such as Uncle Ben's

3 tablespoons butter

1/4 cup chopped onions

1 tablespoon chicken stock base

1/4 teaspoon black pepper

1 1/4 cups hot water

2 tablespoons diced red bell pepper

1/4 cup diced green bell pepper

1. Preheat the oven to 350°F. Rinse the rice in hot water.

2. Melt the butter in a large skillet. Sauté the onions in the butter for about 5 minutes, until tender, then stir in the rice until well coated. Keep warm over very low heat.

3. In a small bowl, mix the chicken stock base and pepper with the hot water, then pour over the rice and stir. Mix in the bell peppers.

4. Place the mixture in a 2- or 3-quart covered casserole or ovenproof pan and bake for 25 to 30 minutes. Serve hot.

Tip: If you wish, throw in a couple of tablespoons of wild rice and bake it a bit longer. You can also add some chopped celery and a couple of chopped scallions as well.

CHAPTER 6 BEANS

Whether you merely open a can of baked beans or hand-picked dried beans to cook in a cast iron saucepan, the members of the bean family are loaded with protein, go well with just about everything, are rich with flavor, and are almost foolproof to cook.

Bodacious Biscuits and Beans

A one-pan dish that's great to serve while watching a football or baseball game— this recipe offers a hearty, delicious, and surprising mixture of textures and tastes. There are few things on earth like home-made biscuits and baked beans loaded with yummy fixin's.

Serves 8 to 10

1 (16-ounce) can baked beans (preferably Bush's Original)

1 (16-ounce) can pinto beans (preferably Bush's), rinsed and drained

1 (16-ounce) can vegetarian baked beans (preferably Bush's), drained

1 (11-ounce) can mandarin orange segments with juice

1 cup golden raisins

1 medium tart apple, such as Granny Smith or Pippin, peeled, cored, and minced

1/2 cup cane syrup or dark molasses

1 small onion, minced

2 tablespoons prepared yellow mustard

1/2 teaspoon ground cinnamon

1/2 teaspoon ground nutmeg

1/2 cup ketchup

2 tablespoons orange juice

1 (10-ounce) package refrigerated biscuits (preferably Pillsbury Grands)

1. Preheat the oven or a grill to 300°F.

2. In a large, ovenproof skillet, gently combine the beans, mandarin oranges, raisins, apple, cane syrup, onions, mustard, spices, ketchup, and orange juice.

3. Cover the skillet with aluminum foil, put into the oven, and bake for 1 hour.

4. Remove the foil, top the beans with the unbaked biscuits, and bake, uncovered, for about 10 minutes longer, or until the biscuits puff up and are browned. Serve from the skillet at the table, giving each person a biscuit and a heaping portion of beans.

Tip: Add 2 cups chopped ham, bacon, or smoked chicken to make this an entrée.

Fava Beans on Little Toasts (Fava Bean Crostini)

The fava bean has been used in Chinese cooking for at least 5,000 years. It was cultivated by almost every ancient society and has been domesticated for so long that there are no wild forms of the bean. This dish could come right out of a fancy food magazine; it's bright green and red colors and variety of textures are as fitting for a luncheon menu or roast beef dinner as they are for an informal backyard barbecue.

Serves 4 to 6

3 tablespoons sun-dried tomatoes

18 to 24 bread slices, 1/4 to 1/2 inch thick (preferably round)

3 tablespoons olive oil

3 cloves garlic, mashed and diced

3 pounds fava beans, shelled

1 teaspoon garlic salt

1 medium, very ripe avocado, coarsely chopped

1 1/2 tablespoons lime or lemon juice

Fresh basil, cut into fine slivers, to serve

1. Soak the sun-dried tomatoes in hot water for 20 minutes, then dice and set aside.

2. Toast the bread briefly, and place it in a warm oven or grill to keep warm.

3. Pour the olive oil into a large saucepan and add the garlic and sun-dried tomatoes, heating the mixture over medium-low heat until the garlic just begins to brown.

4. Add the fava beans and garlic salt, roughly stir the beans and tomatoes to break up the beans. Cover the pan, stir occasionally, and cook until the beans are soft, 15 to 20 minutes.

5. Cool the mixture, then pour it into a food processor and pulse until smooth. Add the avocado and lime juice and pulse briefly. There should still be lumps in the mixture.

6. Spread the avocado-tomato-bean mixture on the warm bread slices and serve hot. Pass a bowl of basil that people can add as they wish.

Tip: The average American eats 15 pounds of beans a year, mostly fresh green (or string) beans or canned pork and beans. Fava beans are more popular in Italy, but they are fast gaining popularity here because they are high in fiber and iron and have no cholesterol.

This dish evolved into baked beans with salt pork and molasses, which became known as Boston baked beans.

Serves 4 to 6

1 cup chopped sweet onion, such as Maui, Walla Walla, or Vidalia

1 tablespoon butter

1/2 pound sliced bacon

1 pound chuck steak, cut into 1-inch pieces

2 (28-ounce) cans baked beans (preferably Bush's Country Style)

1/2 cup dark molasses

1 medium pineapple, stem leaves left on

Sour cream, to serve

1. Place a cast iron skillet over a hot grill or stovetop burner and add the onions and butter, sautéing the onions until slightly browned. Remove the onions from the pan and set aside.

2. Add the bacon to the empty skillet and cook until crisp. Remove the slices, drain on paper towels, and chop into 1-inch pieces; set aside. Pour out half of the bacon fat, retaining the rest in the skillet.

Hawaiian Baked Beans

The Indians of New England were the first to cook and eat baked beans, as they began the practice of digging fire pits in the earth and lining them with stones. The beans were then placed with maple sugar and bear fat inside deer hides and slow-cooked in the pits, later called bean holes.

3. Add the steak to the skillet and brown thoroughly over high heat. When the meat is cooked, add the bacon and stir well. Mix in the beans, molasses, and sautéed onions place on the grill over indirect heat, until the mixture boils, then reduce the heat to maintain a simmer.

4. Cut the pineapple in half vertically, keeping the leaves attached. Lay the pineapple on its round side and remove the inside with a sharp knife or a grapefruit spoon, leaving 1/4 to 1/2 inch at the bottom and sides of the fruit. Take the fruit you remove and loosely chop it into 1/2- to 1-inch cubes.

5. When you are ready to serve the beans, gently fold 1 cup of pineapple into the bean mixture and pour into the two empty pineapple halves.

6. Garnish with the remaining chopped pineapple and a few generous dollops of sour cream; serve.

Tip: Store pineapples at room temperature for 1 to 2 days before serving to allow them to become softer and sweeter. Store whole pineapples in the refrigerator for 3 to 5 days.

Sicilian White Beans and Parmesan

Beans are a great source of vitamin A, thiamin, niacin, folate, and iron and a good source of vitamin C, riboflavin, and calcium. This dish offers white pea beans in a casserole with colorful vegetables, a variety of herbs, and a melted cheese and bread crumb topping.

Serves 8 to 10

2 tablespoons olive oil

2 medium carrots, peeled and diced

2 ribs celery, finely chopped

1 teaspoon minced garlic

1 teaspoon minced shallots

1/4 cup minced fresh parsley

1 medium onion, finely chopped

1 medium orange or yellow
(or green if you must) bell pepper,
seeded and finely chopped

1 (28-ounce) can diced tomatoes with juice

1 (5 1/2-ounce) can tomato paste

3/4 cup dry white wine

1 teaspoon dried basil

1 teaspoon dried savory

1 teaspoon dried oregano

2 teaspoons granulated sugar

1/2 teaspoon sea salt

4 tablespoons grated Parmesan cheese

4 cups cooked white pea beans

1 cup homemade bread crumbs

1/4 cup chopped fresh parsley

2 tablespoons butter, melted

1 cup shredded mozzarella cheese
(about 4 ounces)

1. Preheat the oven to 375°F.

2. In a large pot or Dutch oven, over medium-high heat on a stovetop or grill, heat the olive oil until it just begins to smoke. Add the carrots, celery, garlic, shallots, minced parsley, onions, and bell pepper and sauté until the vegetables are just becoming tender, 8 to 10 minutes.

3. Add the tomatoes, tomato paste, wine, basil, savory, oregano, sugar, salt, and 2 tablespoons of Parmesan cheese, and

bring the mixture to a boil. Reduce the heat and simmer for 20 to 25 minutes, or until thickened.

4. Stir in the beans and cook for 15 minutes longer. While the beans are cooking, combine the bread crumbs, chopped parsley, butter, and the remaining 2 tablespoons Parmesan cheese in a small bowl and set aside.

5. Transfer the cooked bean mixture to a lightly greased 9 x 13-inch baking pan. Sprinkle the top evenly with the mozzarella and then the bread crumb mixture. Bake for 20 to 30 minutes, or until bubbling.

Tip: You can easily make this side into a main dish by adding chopped cooked ham, turkey, or sausage at the same time that you add the tomatoes and paste.

Root Beer BBQ Beans

Everyone loves beans at a barbecue. These have a nice root beer flavor, but you can also use Dr. Pepper, Cherry Coke, or the southern favorite, RC Cola, for a distinctive flavor. Don't use any diet drinks, as they get bitter when cooked.

Serves 4 to 6

5 slices bacon, diced

1 medium onion, diced

1 (36-ounce) can baked beans, preferably Bush's

1 cup root beer (regular, not diet)

2 tablespoons dark molasses

1/2 teaspoon dry mustard

1/4 teaspoon garlic salt

1/4 teaspoon lemon pepper

2 to 3 ribs celery

1. Cook the bacon with the onions in a medium saucepan over a grill or side burner until the bacon is brown and crisp and the onions are just starting to brown and have become transparent.

2. Add the remaining ingredients, including the whole celery ribs.

3. Bring to a boil over medium-high heat, then reduce the heat and simmer, stirring often, until the mixture is slightly thickened, about 20 minutes. Remove the celery and serve the beans hot.

Tip: The celery helps minimize the gaseous effect beans have for some people. Just insert the ribs into the beans while they are cooking, and remove and discard before serving. It works!

Black Bean Bourbon and Honey Pie

This is a rich and hearty bean pie with a sweet touch of honey and the smoky taste of bourbon. Serve it with a strong beer, a large green salad, and a T-bone or sirloin steak.

Serves 8 to 10

1 tablespoon olive oil

1 sweet onion, such as Maui, Walla Walla, or Vidalia, finely chopped

1 medium green bell pepper, seeded and chopped

2 (15-ounce) cans black beans, rinsed and drained

1/3 cup salsa, well drained

1 teaspoon dried oregano

1/4 cup chopped red bell peppers

1 teaspoon chili powder (preferably Mexene)

1/4 teaspoon cayenne pepper

1/2 teaspoon sea salt

1/4 teaspoon black pepper

1/4 cup honey

1/4 cup bourbon

2 (9-inch) pie crusts, unbaked

1 1/2 cups shredded Cheddar cheese (about 6 ounces)

1 pint sour cream

3 tablespoons cinnamon sugar

1. Preheat the oven to 325°F.

2. In a large saucepan over medium heat, heat the oil and sauté the onions and green bell pepper until tender.

3. Add the beans, salsa, oregano, red bell pepper, chili powder, cayenne pepper, salt, pepper, honey, and bourbon. Reduce the heat to low and simmer the mixture for 15 minutes, or until most of the liquid has evaporated.

4. Spoon half of the bean mixture into one of the pie crusts in an aluminum pie plate and cover with half of the cheese. Then spoon the remaining bean mixture on top and cover with the rest of the cheese.

5. Place the second pie crust on top of the pie. Seal the edges by moistening the edge of the bottom pie crust with cold water and pressing a fork onto the joining crusts.

Cut several slits in the top crust to allow steam to escape.

6. Bake for 1 hour, remove from the oven, and let the pie firm up and cool to room temperature. Serve with a dollop of sour cream on each slice, sprinkled with a few dashes of cinnamon sugar.

Tip: You can use rum, whiskey, Scotch, or other favorite sippin' beverage instead of the bourbon; just make sure to evaporate most of the liquid (the flavor stays in the beans, but the alcohol cooks away) in the frying pan.

BBQ Baked Lima Beans

I first learned about these on a trip to Amish country in Pennsylvania. Even folks who say they don't like lima beans will dig into these with glee. They are sometimes called butter beans, especially in the South.

Serves 6 to 8

4 slices bacon, chopped

1 medium onion, diced

8 cups fresh or frozen lima beans

1 cup ketchup

1/2 cup barbecue sauce, preferably Cattlemen's Golden Honey sauce

1/4 cup maple syrup

2 tablespoons dark brown sugar

1/2 teaspoon dry mustard

2 tablespoons prepared yellow mustard

1/4 teaspoon salt

1/4 teaspoon lemon pepper

1. Preheat the oven or grill to 325°F.

2. Cook the bacon with the onions in a large saucepan on the stove or over a grill or side burner until the bacon is brown and crisp and the onions are just starting to brown and have become transparent, 5 to 7 minutes.

3. Pour the onions and bacon into a 2-quart casserole or Dutch oven and add all of the remaining ingredients, stirring to combine.

4. Place the covered casserole in the oven and bake for 1 hour. If the beans are not tender at that time, bake for another 15 to 20 minutes. Serve hot.

Tip: Add 2 cans or bags of frozen corn and you have baked BBQ succotash. DO NOT nibble raw lima beans, as they contain a chemical that releases cyanide when the seed coat is ruptured. Happily, this process is negated by cooking the beans.

Classic

Creamed Fava Beans and Bacon

My grandmother made this dish in northern Ontario, and it was always my favorite when we visited. She adapted this recipe from one she picked up from a library book in the 1940s.

Serves 4

5 pounds young fava beans, in the pods

1/4 pound sliced bacon

1 tablespoon butter

1 branch fresh savory, or pinch of finely crumbled dried savory

2 to 3 tablespoons water, or more as needed

Salt

1/2 cup heavy cream

3 large egg yolks

Black pepper

Lemon juice

Chopped fresh parsley, to serve

1. Shell the beans and remove the skins from all except those pods that are tiny and bright green; set aside.

2. Cut the bacon into 1/2-inch pieces, parboil in a small saucepan for a few seconds to remove excess salt, and drain.

3. Melt the butter in a heavy saucepan over low heat, add the bacon, and cook for 2 to 3 minutes. The bacon should remain limp.

4. Add the fava beans, savory, just enough water to moisten lightly, and salt to taste. Cover tightly and cook over high heat for a few seconds. Turn the heat to low again so the beans stew rather than boil. Cook, occasionally shaking the pan gently, until the beans are tender, 15 to 20 minutes. Remove from the heat, remove the branch of savory, and let cool for 1 to 2 minutes.

5. In a small bowl, mix the cream, egg yolks, and pepper to taste and stir gently into the fava beans. Return to low heat, stirring until the sauce is slightly thickened and coats a spoon thinly. It should not boil. Stir in a few drops of lemon juice to taste, sprinkle with the parsley, and serve.

Tip: In the store, fava bean pods will look a little like giant green beans—long and plump, varying slightly in length, and slightly fuzzy, with some bronzing on the outside of the pod. The stems should be fresh and the pods should be heavy, with just a hint of the rounded beans inside.

Cowboy Pinto Beans

These beans taste like you're on the Chisholm Trail fresh from a cattle drive. They're a bunch of work, but they're worth it, for the flavor is straight from the Old West—other than the Worcestershire sauce, that is.

Serves 6 to 8

1 pound dried pinto beans, debris removed, soaked overnight, and drained (see the Tip)

1/4 pound salt pork

8 cups water, plus more as needed

1 (14-ounce) can whole tomatoes with juice

4 cloves garlic, crushed

1 large onion, chopped

2 tablespoons chili powder

1 teaspoon ground cumin

2 jalapeño chile peppers, seeded and chopped

1 tablespoon Worcestershire sauce

1 cup barbecue sauce or ketchup

1 teaspoon kosher salt

1. Wash and pick over the beans, removing wrinkled or shrunken beans.

2. Make several cuts into the salt pork down to, but not through, the rind.

3. Combine the beans, salt pork, water, tomatoes, garlic, onion, chili powder, cumin, chile peppers, Worcestershire sauce, and barbecue sauce in a heavy saucepan or Dutch oven. Bring to a boil, then reduce the heat to maintain a low simmer. Cook very slowly, covered, stirring the beans up from the bottom occasionally and adding water if they start looking dry.

4. Cook for at least 2 hours. When the beans are soft (not mushy) but still hold their shape, they are done. Serve hot.

Tip: Julia Child's method of soaking beans is to cover them with plenty of water and boil for 2 minutes. Turn off the heat, cover tightly, and let sit for 1 hour. Then drain and cook as usual.

Old-Fashioned Boston Baked Beans

These beans are worth the trouble it takes to make them from scratch, with a rich, full taste that most canned beans can't match. Ask your butcher for salt pork; it's much better than using bacon.

Serves 6 to 8

2 pounds dried white pea beans, rinsed and debris removed

1 teaspoon baking soda

1 pound salt pork

1 medium onion, chopped

1/2 cup sugar

1/2 cup dark molasses

2 teaspoons dry mustard

2 teaspoons salt

1/4 teaspoon black pepper

1. Soak the beans in enough water to cover overnight.

2. In the morning, add the baking soda to the beans and parboil for 10 minutes. Preheat the oven to 350°F.

3. Drain the beans and rinse with cold water.

4. Dice the salt pork into 1-inch squares. Put half with the chopped onion in the bottom of a deep, ovenproof pot.

5. Put the beans in the pot, with the remainder of the salt pork on top. Mix in the remaining ingredients, adding enough hot water to cover.

6. Bake for 6 to 7 hours, adding water as needed to keep the beans moist.

7. Cover the pot, turn off the oven, and leave in the warm oven for up to an hour, until the rest of your meal is ready to serve. Serve hot.

Tip: If you do not wish to use salt pork, use cooked bacon cut into small pieces. Also, you may prefer to use half white sugar and half brown sugar for a richer taste.

American-Style Red Beans and Rice

As either a side dish or a whole meal, combine the creamy pink texture of pinto beans with a whole grain such as rice and you have a virtually fat-free, high-quality protein meal.

Serves 4 to 6

1 pound dried pinto beans

1 large onion, chopped

1 1/2 teaspoons minced garlic

1/2 medium red bell pepper,
seeded and chopped

1 medium ham hock

2 tablespoons tomato paste

2 teaspoons dried oregano

2 teaspoons dried thyme

1/2 teaspoon Louisiana hot sauce

2 cups long-grain white rice

3 cups water

1. Rinse the beans and pick out any stones or debris. Soak the beans overnight in enough water to cover or, if preparing the same day, place them in a pot with water just to cover and bring to a boil. Boil for 2 minutes and turn off the heat. Continue soaking the beans in the cooking water for 1 hour.

2. Add the onion, garlic, red pepper, ham hock, tomato paste, oregano, thyme, and hot sauce to the soaked beans, cover, and bring to a boil. Turn the heat down and cook over medium heat for 1 hour.

3. Remove the ham hock, trim away the fatty skin, remove the meat from the bone, and discard the bone. Chop the meat into small pieces and return to the pot. Continue cooking for 1 hour. The liquid will have boiled down to a thick, brown sauce, and the beans should be soft but not mushy. Take off the heat and set aside.

4. Place the rice and 3 cups water in a medium saucepan. Cover and bring to a boil. Without uncovering, reduce the heat to maintain a simmer and cook for 18 minutes. Turn off the heat and allow the rice to rest for 5 minutes. Serve the beans over the rice.

Tip: Store dried beans in an airtight container in a cool, dry, and dark place, where they will keep for up to 12 months. Cooked pinto beans will keep in the refrigerator for about 3 days, if placed in a covered container.

Southern Succotash

I detested this dish as a kid, but I have learned to enjoy it and cook it often when friends come over for barbecue. The meaty lima beans blend nicely with the crisp corn in their bath of cream sauce.

Serves 4 to 6

2 cups fresh or frozen lima beans

2 cups fresh, frozen, or canned corn (about 16 ounces)

2 tablespoons butter

1 teaspoon salt

Dash of black pepper

1 teaspoon sugar

1/2 cup water

1/4 cup heavy cream

1. If using fresh lima beans, cook in boiling salted water until tender. If using frozen beans, cook according to the package instructions.

2. In a medium saucepan, mix the cooked beans with the corn (drained if using canned), butter, salt, pepper, sugar, and water. Simmer over low heat for 10 to 15 minutes.

3. Drain, add the cream, and heat until hot, but do not boil. Serve immediately.

Tip: Some folks add stewed tomatoes and onions to this, but that overpowers the subtle flavors of the beans and corn. And while the tomato and onion version is good, it's more a vegetable stew than succotash.

Montego Bay Rice and Beans

This dish goes very well with barbecued chicken, especially if you "jerk" your chicken, rubbing fiery Jamaican spices into and under the skin before grilling. Here's a simple "jerk" recipe: Mix 1 teaspoon each of the following: onion powder, dried thyme, ground allspice, ground cinnamon, black pepper, cayenne pepper, salt, and ground nutmeg. Add 2 teaspoons sugar.

Serves 6 to 8

1 (16-ounce) can large red kidney beans, rinsed and drained

2 to 2 1/2 cups water

1 (16-ounce) can unsweetened coconut milk

2 cups long-grain white rice

2 cloves garlic, chopped

1 teaspoon salt

2 scallions, chopped

1/2 teaspoon black pepper

1 sprig fresh thyme

1/2 teaspoon hot pepper sauce, such as Tabasco

1. In a large saucepan, combine all of the ingredients and bring to a boil.

2. Reduce the heat and simmer for 20 to 25 minutes, until all the liquid is absorbed.

3. Stir well and serve hot.

Tip: Unless you are making risotto, you should rarely stir rice while it is cooking, as you can easily crush the delicate grains and release the starch, which will make the rice gummy and sticky.

CHAPTER 7 SALSAS

Spice up your life! Salsas offer fresh fruit, fresh veggies, tart vinegars, and zippy spices all blended in bright bowls to dip into, to spoon over fish or poultry, or to use as a side dish that wakes up the taste buds.

Banana Boat Salsa

Every year Americans eat more than 30 pounds of bananas, more than any other fruit. Good thing each contains only 0.6 grams of fat. This salsa is wonderful with fish steaks or fillets, and provides pleasant diversion on a hot afternoon. Make sure the bananas are coated with the lime juice so they don't turn brown in the bowl.

Makes 2 cups

1 large firm banana, slightly underripe, peeled and diced

1/2 cup diced red bell pepper

1/2 cup diced yellow bell pepper

3 tablespoons chopped fresh cilantro

2 scallions, chopped

2 tablespoons lime juice

1 tablespoon brown sugar

1 teaspoon minced fresh ginger

2 teaspoons olive oil

1/4 teaspoon crushed red pepper flakes

Salt and pepper

1. In a medium, nonreactive bowl, mix the banana, bell peppers, cilantro, scallions, lime juice, brown sugar, ginger, olive oil, and red pepper flakes. Stir well. Taste and add salt and pepper if you wish.

2. Let the salsa sit for 15 minutes to absorb the flavors and serve immediately. Any longer and the banana gets too mushy.

Tip: This salsa is best served with fish or pork dishes. Try it alongside halibut fillets or fresh trout.

Avocado and Roasted Tomatillo Salsa

This salsa has a tomato taste that is made very rich by the mashed avocado and the bite of jalapeño. It is excellent with grilled shrimp, fish, or chicken.

Makes 3 cups

1/2 pound tomatillos (6 to 8 medium tomatillos)

1/2 small onion

2 cloves garlic, unpeeled

2 tablespoons chopped fresh cilantro

1 teaspoon salt

1 jalapeño chile pepper

1 1/2 medium avocados, peeled and pitted

1. Preheat a grill or broiler to high heat.

2. Remove the husks from the tomatillos and rinse under warm water to remove the stickiness.

3. Cut the onion in half and place it on the grill or broiler rack with the tomatillos and garlic. Grill or broil 1 to 2 inches from the heat, turning once, until softened and slightly charred, about 10 minutes. Set aside.

4. Peel the garlic and put it in a food processor with the tomatillos, onion, cilantro, and salt.

5. Chop the chile pepper, discarding the seeds and stem, and add to the tomatillo mixture. Pulse until the mixture is smooth but still has lumps. Transfer to a nonreactive bowl.

6. Spoon the avocado flesh into the bowl and, with a fork, mash the avocado into the mixture, leaving a lumpy texture.

7. Let the salsa sit, refrigerated, for 30 minutes to marry the flavors, then serve chilled or at room temperature.

Tip: Tomatillos are small fruits (used as a vegetable) enclosed in a papery husk. The fruit resembles a small, unripe tomato and is usually green or yellow. When shopping, select tomatillos that have an intact, tight-fitting, light brown husk. Under the skin the fruit should be firm and free of blemishes.

Blueberry-Grapefruit Salsa

Use only fresh blueberries in this. Frozen or canned ones don't work very well and have a poor consistency. Made with pink grapefruit, red onions, jalapeño chile peppers, honey, lime juice, and fresh cilantro, this salsa delivers lots of lively flavor.

Makes 2 to 3 cups

1 large pink grapefruit

2 tablespoons finely chopped red onion

1 jalapeño chile pepper, seeded and chopped

1 teaspoon honey

1 tablespoon lime juice

1 cup blueberries

2 tablespoons chopped fresh cilantro

1. Peel and section the grapefruit and discard the membranes.

2. Dice the grapefruit and mix with the remaining ingredients in a medium, non-reactive bowl. Let sit for 30 minutes to blend the flavors. Serve at room temperature.

Tip: This salsa is incredible on grilled salmon or halibut.

Tropical Citrus-Apple Salsa

I invented this salsa to be served at the Monterey Bay Aquarium's Sustainable Seafood event. The fish I was asked to cook was trout, and this tangy, crisp, and fresh salsa went extremely well with the boned, butterflied trout fillets. The rum was added at the very last minute in a burst of inspiration.

Makes 3 cups

4 medium tart apples, such as Granny Smith or Pippin, unpeeled, cored, and finely diced

2 teaspoons finely chopped orange zest

1 teaspoon finely chopped lemon zest

1 teaspoon finely chopped lime zest

1/4 cup pineapple rum

1 teaspoon finely minced jalapeño chile pepper

1/4 cup finely chopped fresh cilantro

6 scallions, thinly sliced

1 (8-ounce) can cranberry jelly

Salt and pepper

In a large, nonreactive bowl, combine all of the ingredients, including salt and pepper to taste, and chill for at least 30 minutes.

Tip: Granny Smith or Pippin apples have the right amount of tang for this dish. Other varieties may be too bland and have less crunch in the final product.

Kiwi and Pear Salsa

Kiwi, jalapeño, and pear? Oh my! Such different flavors that go so well together —this is a surprising salsa that is super with fish and fish tacos.

Makes 2 cups

1 large orange

1 medium lime

1 medium lemon

1 to 3 jalapeño chile peppers, seeded

3 medium kiwifruit, peeled

1 medium firm pear, peeled and cored

1 teaspoon sugar

2 tablespoons white wine vinegar

Salt

1. Grate the zest from the orange, lime, and lemon, then squeeze the juice from each of these fruits into a small, nonreactive bowl.

2. Finely chop the chile peppers and add to the bowl.

3. Pour into a food processor and add the kiwifruit, pear, sugar, and vinegar, pulsing until you still have chunks but the mixture has some smoothness as well. Season to taste with salt.

4. Before serving, chill in a nonreactive container for at least 30 minutes to let the flavors become richer.

Tip: This fresh, fruity salsa is also great with roast pork or chicken.

Pomegranate and Orange Salsa

I'll bet you didn't know that the pomegranate is one of the oldest known fruits on earth, and in Europe it has a bit of unusual history. The first pomegranate planted in Britain was by none other than King Henry VIII. Next door, the French named their hand-tossed explosive a grenade after the seed-scattering properties of the pomegranate fruit. This bright, zesty, and colorful salsa goes especially well with any kind of poultry or fish.

Makes 3 cups

1 large pomegranate

2 large oranges, peeled and deveined

1 jalapeño chile pepper, seeded and minced

1 large tomato, peeled, seeded, and chopped

2 tablespoons thinly sliced scallions

1 tablespoon lime juice

1 tablespoon minced fresh cilantro

1/2 teaspoon ground cumin

Salt and pepper

1. Break the pomegranate apart to release the seeds. Discard the membranes and the skin.

2. Wash and drain the seeds, pat dry with paper towels, then place in a medium, nonreactive bowl.

3. Add the oranges, chile pepper, tomato, scallions, lime juice, cilantro, and cumin. Stir well, then add salt and pepper to taste.

4. Cover and chill for at least 2 hours before serving.

Tip: This salsa goes especially well with seafood, including shrimp, scallops, crab, and firm-fleshed fish.

Grilled Corn Salsa

Columbus not only "discovered" America, he reported on a new vegetable he'd seen in Cuba: "My party had seen many fields... also of a grain like panic-grass that the Indians call maize. This grain has a very good taste when cooked, either roasted or ground and made into a gruel." And the fresher the corn, the better. After you cut off the grilled kernels for this recipe, use the back of the knife to milk the juice off the ear. Serve alongside hot pork chops, roast pork, or pulled, barbecued pork.

Makes 3 to 4 cups

2 teaspoons olive oil

1 (15-ounce) can black beans, rinsed and drained

2 large tomatoes, peeled (optional) and cut into large chunks

1 large avocado, peeled, pitted, and cut into large chunks

2 jalapeño chile peppers, seeded and minced

2 tablespoons lime juice

1/4 cup chopped fresh cilantro

1/2 teaspoon salt

2 medium ears corn

1. Have medium-hot coals ready, or preheat a gas grill.

2. In a large, nonreactive bowl, combine the beans, tomatoes, avocado, corn, chile peppers, lime juice, cilantro, and salt. Set aside.

3. Remove the husks and silks from the corn and grill until the kernels start to lightly brown in spots. Remove the corn from the grill, cut off the kernels, and add to the salsa.

4. Let the mixture rest at room temperature for at least 30 minutes, stirring occasionally, and serve.

Tip: The flavor of grilled corn really makes this dish special, but if you can't grill it as above, there is a stovetop option. Cut the kernels off the ear, add to a small skillet with 1 tablespoon oil, and fry lightly over high heat for 3 to 4 minutes. Add to the salsa and complete the recipe as directed.

Black Bean and Papaya Salsa

This Caribbean-inspired salsa is great with grilled fish and also makes a spicy summer-salad-type course.

Makes 3 1/2 cups

1 cup cooked or canned black beans (rinse and drain if using canned)

2 medium papayas, peeled, seeded, and diced small

1/2 medium red bell pepper, seeded and diced small

1/2 medium green bell pepper, seeded and diced small

1/2 medium red onion, diced small

3/4 cup pineapple juice

1/2 cup lime juice (from about 4 limes)

1/2 cup chopped fresh cilantro

2 tablespoons ground cumin

1 tablespoon minced red or green chile pepper of your choice

Salt

Cracked black pepper

In a large, nonreactive bowl, combine all the ingredients, including salt and cracked pepper to taste, and mix together well. This salsa will keep, covered and refrigerated, for 4 to 5 days.

Tip: There are two kinds of papaya, Hawaiian and Mexican. The Hawaiian ones, also known as Solo papayas, are the ones most commonly found in supermarkets. They are pear shaped, weigh about a pound each, and have yellow skin when ripe. The Mexican papayas can be found in Latino markets. These can weigh up to 20 pounds and be more than 15 inches long. Their flavor is less intense than the Hawaiian papaya.

Classic
Chipotle Chile Salsa

Chipotles are smoked jalapeño chile peppers, also known as *chile ahumado*. They are smoked because the thick, fleshy jalapeño is difficult to dry and prone to rot. As much as one fifth of the Mexican jalapeño crop is processed into chipotles. This salsa has a bit of fire, which you can tone up or down by adding more or fewer chile peppers. You can also add honey instead of brown sugar for a different level of sweetness.

Makes 2 cups

3 chipotle chile peppers, rinsed and drained

6 to 8 tomatillos

1/4 cup chopped onion

1 tablespoon snipped fresh thyme

1 teaspoon minced garlic

1 teaspoon brown sugar

1/4 teaspoon salt

1. Cut the chile peppers open and discard the stems and seeds. Chop into 1/4-inch pieces, place in a small bowl, and cover with boiling water. Let stand for 45 to 60 minutes to soften, then drain well and set aside.

2. Remove the husks from the tomatillos, rinse under warm water to remove the stickiness, and finely chop; you should have about 2 cups.

3. In a medium, nonreactive bowl, combine the chile peppers, tomatillos, onions, thyme, garlic, brown sugar, and salt.

4. Cover the salsa and let stand at room temperature for 30 minutes to blend the flavors; serve.

Tip: Serve this salsa as a dip for chips or as a condiment for grilled steaks, roasts, chicken, or fish.

Fresh Salsa (Salsa Fresca)

This recipe is similar to one listed in a 1950s cookbook I have in my library. Its strengths are in the fresh, fresh ingredients used and the fact that you can make it and be ready to serve it in 10 minutes. The clean, fresh taste goes well with pita bread or tortilla chips, or with broiled fish or chicken.

Makes 2 to 3 cups

2 cloves garlic

1/2 medium onion, quartered

1 to 2 jalapeño chile peppers or other small hot chile peppers, seeded

1/4 cup chopped fresh cilantro

1 pound tomatoes, seeded and coarsely chopped

2 tablespoons salad oil

Juice of 1 lime

Salt and pepper

1. Mince the garlic, onion, and chile peppers and combine in a large, nonreactive bowl.

2. Add the cilantro and tomatoes to the bowl, mix well, then stir in the oil and lime juice. Season to taste with salt and pepper and serve.

Tip: You can make this in a food processor for a moister (less chunky) texture. But don't over-mix or you'll get salsa soup.

Classic
Tomatillo Salsa (Salsa Verde)

This classic Veracruz-style salsa is great as a dip with chips and pita bread, but it's even better on grilled chicken, fish, or steaks! The avocado adds a smooth contrast to the bite of the chiles and onion.

Makes 2 cups

2 cloves garlic, cut into large chunks

1 1/2 teaspoons salt, or to taste

1 small white onion, coarsely chopped

2 to 3 serrano chile peppers, or to taste, seeded and cut into large chunks

1/2 pound tomatillos (6 to 8 medium tomatillos), husks removed, rinsed, and cut into quarters

4 to 6 sprigs fresh cilantro

1 ripe Mexican-type avocado (preferably Hass or Fuerte)

1. In a food processor or blender, process the garlic and salt to a paste.

2. Scrape down the sides, if necessary, with a rubber spatula; add the onions, chile peppers, tomatillos, and cilantro, and process with an on-off motion to make a slightly chunky purée.

3. Scoop the avocado flesh into the machine and process to desired smoothness. Serve within 1 hour (or preferably at once) in a nonreactive bowl.

Tip: You can use a sweet white onion if you wish, but most people prefer the sharp taste of a less sweet variety.

CHAPTER 8 POTATOES

They're called spuds or taters, they're yellow and red and white and even blue, and we fry, boil, broil, barbecue, shred, bake, roast, sauté, mash, and smoke them to come up with yummy sides that a picnic wouldn't be a picnic without.

Asian Fusion Potato Pancakes

Here's a pancake dish using Asian sauce that will liven up any breakfast, but especially one featuring sausage and eggs. For that matter, try a dinner of grilled bratwurst, coleslaw, and these tasty pancakes.

Serves 6 to 8

Sauce:

2 tablespoons chopped scallions

2 tablespoons soy sauce

1 teaspoon toasted sesame seeds

1 tablespoon sesame oil

1/2 teaspoon nuoc nam (Vietnamese fish sauce)

1 tablespoon brown sugar

1 teaspoon finely chopped garlic

1 teaspoon finely chopped fresh ginger

1 pound frozen shredded hash brown potatoes, thawed, or 1 pound shredded waxy potatoes, such as thin-skinned red or white

1 large egg, beaten

1 tablespoon all-purpose flour

3 scallions, cut into 2-inch-long slivers

1. Preheat a grill or stovetop burner to medium-high.

2. To make the sauce, mix together the scallions, soy sauce, sesame seeds, sesame oil, nuoc nam, brown sugar, garlic, and ginger in a large bowl. Set aside.

3. Make sure the potatoes are well drained, squeezing any water out of them (especially if you've made your own using a grating blade in a food processor).

4. Place the potatoes in a large bowl and add the egg, flour, and scallions, mixing with your hands until thoroughly mixed.

5. Using cooking oil or nonstick cooking spray, grease a large, nonstick skillet and place it over the heat. When a drop of water sizzles, the oil is ready.

6. Measure 1/4 cup of the potato-onion mixture and press firmly into a ball, then flatten it in your hand to form a pancake abut 1/2 inch thick. Repeat until you have made all of the mixture into pancakes.

7. Cook 3 to 4 pancakes in the skillet at a time, without crowding. When they are golden brown on the bottom, turn over with a spatula and brown the second side. The total cooking time should be about 8 minutes per pancake.

8. Remove the cooked pancakes to a tray in a warm oven and keep quite hot. Serve with a spoonful of the sauce poured over each pancake, or serve the sauce on the side.

Tip: Try adding 2 cups shredded apple (sprinkled with lemon juice so it won't turn brown) along with the potato and onions. You will probably have to add one more large egg as well.

Classic
Velveeta Au Gratin

Don't laugh. There are two ways to use Velveeta cheese that are memorable. The first is in this dish, and the second is in grilled cheese sandwiches. Sure, other fancy cheeses taste wonderful, but for the memories of my youth, nothing cuts it like good ol' Velveeta.

Serves 4 to 6

5 cups peeled and thinly sliced Yukon Gold potatoes (5 to 6 medium)

1/2 pound Velveeta cheese, cubed

1/2 cup chopped onion

1 teaspoon dry mustard

1/4 teaspoon black pepper

1/4 cup milk

1. Preheat the oven to 350°F.

2. Cook the potatoes in boiling water in a large saucepan for 8 to 10 minutes, or until they are fork-tender; drain.

3. Toss the potatoes with the remaining ingredients in a buttered (or sprayed) 2-quart casserole and cover.

4. Bake for 22 to 25 minutes, or until the potatoes are tender. Stir gently before serving.

Tip: If you must, you can substitute Swiss, Gruyère, or imported Cheddar for the "cheese in a box." But I wouldn't.

Buttered and Baked Potatoes

This very simple, almost foolproof dish brings out the delicate taste of potatoes with the help of rosemary sprigs and black pepper. Use butter only—no substitutes— and don't stint on the quality of the butter you buy. Only the best is good enough for this dish, and your hungry guests.

Serves 4

1 1/2 pounds very small potatoes (such as fingerlings or new potatoes)

3 tablespoons butter, melted

1/2 teaspoon sea salt or kosher salt

4 large sprigs fresh rosemary

Black pepper

1. Preheat the oven or grill to 375°F.

2. Under running water, scrub the potatoes to remove soil or other debris. If the potatoes are very small, use them whole. Otherwise cut them into 1 1/2- to 2-inch pieces.

3. Place the potatoes in a Dutch oven, medium casserole, or 2-quart baking dish, in one layer.

4. In a large bowl, pour the butter over the rosemary, add the salt, and mix lightly.

5. Pour the butter and rosemary over the potatoes and stir until well coated. Cover the pan with a lid or with tightly wrapped aluminum foil.

6. Bake for 40 minutes, stirring several times, until the potatoes are tender all the way through.

7. Turn the oven heat to 425°F, or increase the gas burners of the grill to reach that temperature. Uncover the pan, place back in the oven, and cook for about 20 minutes, stirring often, until the potatoes are browned on all sides.

8. Remove the rosemary sprigs, give the potatoes a healthy dash of pepper, and serve piping hot, right from the pan.

Tip: Butter, and slow cooking, is the secret to this perfect potato dish. Splurge and buy some French Beurre de Baratte, salted Beurre d'Echire, or Beurre d'Isigny. If your market can't get these, go to www.gourmetfoodstore.com and bring your wallet.

Garlic and Parmesan Spuds

Potatoes were highly prized, and priced, during the Alaskan Klondike gold rush, (1897–1898) and were almost worth their weight in gold as miners, desperate for vitamin C, traded gold for bags of spuds. The addition of Parmesan cheese in this dish makes these buttery potatoes almost illegal—they're so delicious. Then when you add the cream and fresh basil…well this must be what they serve in heaven!

Serves 4 to 6

6 large russet or Yukon Gold potatoes

5 cloves garlic, crushed

1/2 cup (1 stick) butter, melted

1/4 teaspoon coarse or kosher salt

1/2 teaspoon white pepper

1 tablespoon chopped fresh basil

4 cups chicken stock

4 cups heavy cream

1/2 cup grated Parmesan cheese

1. Preheat the oven to 350°F. Cut the potatoes in half lengthwise and then, with the cut side lying flat on a cutting board, make cuts three fourths of the way through at every 1/4 inch along the length. Place flat side down in a greased 2-quart casserole dish.

2. In a small bowl, mix the garlic, butter, salt, pepper, and basil and pour over the potatoes, making sure the butter gets inside the cuts. Pour the chicken stock into the pan, but NOT over the potatoes.

3. Cover the pan with aluminum foil and bake for 35 minutes, or until the potatoes are soft.

4. Gently pour off the chicken stock, then pour in the cream and sprinkle the potatoes generously with the Parmesan cheese.

5. Bake for another 10 minutes, and serve.

Tip: Have trouble mincing or chopping garlic? Place the whole cloves on a cutting board and, using the flat part of a wide or French knife (or Chinese cleaver), smash the cloves until flat. The papery skin then peels off easily, and the garlic clove is easy to chop or mince.

Brandied Mushrooms on Mashed Yukon Gold Cakes

These potato cakes go wonderfully with roast beef or pork, and with oven or barbecue-roasted chicken. Add corn on the cob, or fresh green beans sautéed with bacon and onion, and you have a feast.

Serves 4

Mashed potatoes:

2 pounds Yukon Gold potatoes, peeled (optional) and quartered

1 pound sweet potatoes, quartered

2 large eggs, beaten

Salt and pepper

2 cups dry bread crumbs

Mushroom gravy:

8 cups mushrooms, such as morels, cremini, or chanterelles (about 1/2 pound)

1 teaspoon butter

1 tablespoon olive oil

1 sprig fresh thyme

1 teaspoon minced garlic

1 shallot, finely chopped

1/4 cup brandy

1 1/2 cups evaporated skim milk
(about 12 ounces)

1 teaspoon salt

1/4 teaspoon black pepper

2 tablespoons lemon juice

1 teaspoon dried savory

1 tablespoon olive oil

Chopped fresh parsley, to serve (optional)

Crumbled crisp bacon, to serve (optional)

Sprigs of fresh thyme, to serve (optional)

1. To make the mashed potatoes, boil the potatoes in a large pot of salted water until they are soft, about 20 minutes. Drain well and mash with the eggs. The mixture shouldn't be too moist. Season to taste with salt and pepper.

2. Divide and form the mashed potatoes into 6 to 8 cakes, or patties, and dip the cakes into the bread crumbs. Set aside.

3. To make the gravy, clean and trim the mushrooms and set aside.

4. In a large frying pan over low heat, melt the butter and oil, then add the thyme, garlic, and shallot. Sauté for about 2 minutes, then add the mushrooms and cook, covered, for 5 minutes.

5. Turn the heat to medium-high and stir, uncovered, until the mushrooms brown and the liquid has nearly evaporated. Remove the pan from the heat and carefully stir in the brandy. Add the evaporated milk, salt, pepper, lemon juice, and savory, then return the pan to medium heat and stir until all the liquid is evaporated. Remove the thyme sprig, cover, and keep warm.

6. While you're reducing the gravy, spray a frying pan with nonstick cooking spray, add 1 tablespoon olive oil, and sauté the mashed potato cakes until brown on both sides and heated through.

7. Place a cake on each plate and spoon the mushroom mixture over the top. Garnish with parsley, bacon pieces, and/or more thyme sprigs.

Tip: If you can't find Yukon Gold potatoes, try these varieties: Bintje (a Dutch heirloom potato), German Butterball, Carola, or Charlotte. All are golden to tan skinned and cook up creamy and flavorful.

Dutch Oven Cheese Taters

This dish, with its rich sauce of Cheddar cheese, blue cheese, and sour cream, can be prepared in the oven or in a grill. Note that ham can be substituted for the bacon, as can chopped or pulled pork, or Canadian bacon pieces.

Serves 4 to 6

1 pound bacon, or 1 pound smoked ham, cut into 1/2-inch cubes

5 pounds waxy potatoes, such as thin-skinned red or white

3 to 4 medium onions

1 tablespoon paprika

1 teaspoon dried savory

1 teaspoon minced garlic

Salt and pepper

1/2 pound sharp Cheddar cheese, shredded (about 2 cups)

1/2 pound blue cheese, crumbled

1 pint sour cream

1. Preheat the oven to 350°F.

2. Chop the bacon into 1/2-inch pieces and fry in a 12-inch Dutch oven or cast iron pot over medium-high heat until very crisp.

3. While the bacon is cooking, peel and slice the potatoes (approximately 1/2-inch slices) and coarsely chop the onions.

4. Remove the bacon from the Dutch oven and set aside, leaving the grease in the pot.

5. Add the onions to the bacon grease and cook over medium heat until they begin to be transparent, about 10 minutes.

6. Add the potatoes, bacon, paprika, savory, garlic, and salt and pepper to taste, and stir to coat the potatoes with bacon grease and incorporate the spices.

7. Place the lid on the Dutch oven, and bake for 1 hour.

8. Remove the pot from the oven and carefully lift the lid, as steam will rise out of the pot and can burn. Fold in the Cheddar cheese, blue cheese, and sour cream, and serve.

Tip: If using ham cubes, pulled pork, or Canadian bacon pieces instead of bacon, lightly brown the meat in 1/4 cup olive oil. Remove the meat, leaving the oil in the pot to sauté the onions, then add the meat, potatoes, and other ingredients as described in the recipe.

Salt-Pack *Pertaiters*

This is an easy way to cook delicious spuds. The little guys come out all wrinkly, like a baby's skin after a bath, but they're tender, and the salt adds a nice flavor that (surprise) is not salty!

Serves 6 to 8

1 to 2 pounds small red potatoes

4 to 6 cups kosher or sea salt (or a mix), plus more as needed

Sour cream, to serve

Salmon roe (eggs) or caviar, to serve

1. Preheat the oven or grill to 400°F.

2. Spread a 1/2-inch layer of salt in a Dutch oven or heavy, 2-quart casserole dish. Place the potatoes on the salt and completely cover them with more salt so they are covered by at least 1/2 inch.

3. Place the pot in the oven and cook for about an hour, or until the potatoes are tender all the way through. Poke a knife through the salt, deep into the potatoes, to check for doneness.

4. Dump the potatoes and salt onto a large baking sheet, remove the potatoes, and save the salt to use in this dish again.

5. Cut the cooked potatoes in half lengthwise and serve with a dollop of sour cream and a teaspoon of salmon roe, or caviar if you've just won the lottery. Serve hot.

Tip: If your casserole dish or Dutch oven is 4 inches deep or more, you can do this in two layers. Just add more salt and more potatoes.

Rum-Glazed Sweet Potatoes

The only festival in America devoted to the sweet potato is the Benton, Kentucky, three-day Tater Day Festival, which had its beginnings in 1843. Southerners especially love the sweet taters, among the most nutritious vegetables on the planet, packed with calcium, potassium, and vitamins A and C. This recipe adds spice to the sweet, first coating sweet potato slices in jerk seasoning before grilling and topping with the glaze.

Serves 6

Jerk seasoning:

1 tablespoon onion powder

2 teaspoons ground thyme

2 teaspoons salt

1 teaspoon ground allspice

1/4 teaspoon ground nutmeg

1/4 teaspoon ground cinnamon

2 teaspoons sugar

1 teaspoon coarsely ground black pepper

1 teaspoon cayenne pepper

Pinch of ground cloves

4 large sweet potatoes, peeled and sliced 1/2 inch thick

Glaze:

1/4 cup dark molasses

1/4 cup dark rum (preferably pineapple rum)

1/2 cup dark brown sugar

3/4 cup golden raisins

2 tablespoons butter, softened

1. Preheat a grill to medium-low.

2. To make the jerk seasoning, mix the ingredients in a small bowl. Place the sweet potato slices in a resealable plastic bag, spray with nonstick cooking spray, and add the jerk seasoning, reserving 1 teaspoon for the glaze. Toss well to coat.

3. Place the slices on the grill over direct heat and let cook over low heat until they start to brown, about 4 minutes. Turn over and grill the other side. When both sides are browned, move the slices to the indirect heat side of the grill and cover the grill.

4. To prepare the glaze, combine the molasses, rum, brown sugar, raisins, and reserved 1 teaspoon jerk seasoning in a small sauce-pan. Heat over medium-high heat and let simmer for 10 minutes. Remove from the heat, swirl in the butter, and stir well.

5. Place the grilled sweet potatoes in a large bowl and add the glaze, tossing to coat thoroughly. Serve with grilled flank or hanger steak, pork chops, chicken, or fish.

Tip: Sweet potatoes come in two varieties: the dry-fleshed yellow kind and the plumper orange kind. Most southerners prefer the latter because of its sweetness and moister flesh.

Creamy New Potatoes and Peas

This is cheating! Not only is this classic Maine side dish great on the side, with roast chicken or even the classic Maine red hot dog, but it's incredible as the whole meal. Just be sure to get the newest, freshest-from-the-field potatoes and peas that you can.

Serves 4 to 6

1 pound small new potatoes

1 teaspoon salt

1/2 pound peas

2/3 cup heavy cream

1/2 cup (1 stick) butter

Salt and pepper

1. Thoroughly clean the potatoes, leave the skin on, cut in half, and cook in 2 cups salted boiling water until almost tender.

2. In a separate pot of salted water, cook the shelled peas until just starting to become tender.

3. Serve bowls of peas and potatoes, along with a pitcher of the cream and the butter at the table.

4. Take 3 or 4 potatoes and roughly mash them on your plate. Dab the spuds generously with butter, add 3 or 4 heaping tablespoons of cooked peas, drizzle cream over the top, and season to taste with salt and pepper. Dig in and enjoy!

Tip: If you can't get new potatoes right from a farmer's market or roadside stand, buy the small red potatoes. And if you can't find fresh peas to shell, a poor but okay substitute is frozen peas. Do not under any circumstances use canned peas, or I will hunt you down.

Smoke-Baked Taters

Although the United States consumes a whopping 145 pounds of potatoes per person each year (before the Atkins craze, that is), we're potato pikers compared to the rest of the world—not even in the top 10 consumer nations. Belarus, in the former Soviet Republic, leads the pack, with each citizen chomping down 420 pounds of the starchy vegetable every year. Fortunately, the smoky, herbed taste of this grilled potato recipe is delicious enough to keep us in the running!

Serves 4 to 6

1 handful soaked wood chips (hickory, oak, apple, etc.)

6 large russet or Yukon Gold potatoes

1/2 cup bacon grease (from 6 to 8 slices bacon)

1 tablespoon coarse or kosher salt

1 tablespoon white pepper

1 tablespoon dried basil

1 tablespoon dried sage

1 tablespoon paprika

Butter, to serve

Sour cream, to serve

Chopped fresh chives or green onions, to serve

1. Preheat a grill to 375°F. Cut a 12 x 12-inch sheet of heavy-duty aluminum foil and place the soaked wood chips on it. Fold it into an envelope and poke 3 holes in the top with a pencil. Place the packet directly on the charcoal or gas flame in the grill.

2. Cut the potatoes in half lengthwise, but do not peel them.

3. If you are dainty, brush the potatoes with melted bacon grease (it's best if the grease has just begun to thicken up). Otherwise, use your hands and massage the grease into the potato halves. Set aside in a large bowl.

4. On a large piece of aluminum foil, mix the salt, pepper, basil, sage, and paprika with a spoon, then roll each potato half in the spices until well coated on all sides.

5. Place the potatoes, flat side down, over direct heat for 5 to 10 minutes, just long enough to get some browning and leave grill marks.

6. Turn the potatoes over and cook, skin side down, over indirect heat for approximately 40 minutes, until soft all the way through.

7. Turn the potatoes, flat side down, if they need more browning; otherwise remove them to a heated platter. Serve with butter, sour cream, and freshly chopped chives.

Tip: These are great with grilled rib-eye steaks, prime rib, or beer-butt chicken. They can also be cooked in an oven, but you'd best leave the aluminum foil and wood chips outside.

Vidalias Au Gratin

The story of these sweet onions began in 1931, in Toombs County, Georgia, when a farmer named Coleman discovered that the onions he had planted were not hot, as he had anticipated, but sweet! He sold the onions for $3.50 per 50-pound bag, a big price in the Great Depression, and many other farmers began growing the crop. The onions sold out of a local farmer's market in the city of Vidalia, and word soon got around about "Vidalia onions." This recipe's rich combination of potatoes, sweet onions, and cheese would surely make Farmer Coleman smile.

Serves 4

2 cups cooked waxy potatoes, such as thin-skinned red or white, peeled and sliced

1 cup chopped sweet Vidalia onions or any other sweet variety

1/3 cup butter or margarine

3 tablespoons all-purpose flour

1 1/2 cups milk

3/4 teaspoon salt

1 teaspoon black pepper

1/2 teaspoon granulated garlic, or to taste

1/2 cup shredded Cheddar cheese

1/2 cup shredded Gouda cheese

Paprika, to serve

1. Preheat the oven to 350°F. Combine the potatoes and onions in a greased 1-quart casserole and set aside.

2. In a medium saucepan, melt the butter over medium heat, then stir in the flour until smooth. Gradually add the milk, stirring constantly, until the mixture thickens and begins to bubble. Add the salt, pepper, and garlic, then gradually blend in the cheeses, stirring until the mixture is uniform and smooth.

3. Pour the cheese sauce over the potato mixture and stir once or twice to mix. Sprinkle paprika lightly over the potatoes.

4. Bake for 40 minutes, or until bubbly and beginning to brown on top. Serve hot.

Tip: For a stronger cheese flavor, mix Cheddar and blue cheese, or use Huntsman, a blend of Double Gloucester and blue cheese.

German Potatoes

Grilled bratwurst or knockwurst, with red cabbage, sauerkraut, and heaps of hot German potato salad—it's a memorable meal I repeated many times on a trip down Germany's Romantiche Strasse (romantic highway with my wife Kathy). Try these once and you'll be hooked on the interplay of tart and sweet, tender and crunchy, and overwhelmed by the scent as the dish comes to the table.

Serves 4 to 6

8 medium waxy potatoes, such as thin-skinned red or white

6 to 8 slices bacon

1/2 to 3/4 cup chopped onion

Dressing:

2 1/2 to 3 tablespoons all-purpose flour

1 1/2 cups hot chicken stock

1/2 cup cider vinegar

1 1/2 tablespoons sugar

1 teaspoon salt

1/2 teaspoon black pepper, or more to taste

1 teaspoon dry mustard

1. Cover the potatoes with cold water and bring to a boil. Reduce the heat and cook gently as you prepare the rest of the dish. Keep an eye on them, as you only want to cook until just tender.

2. As the potatoes cook, fry the bacon until crisp and drain, reserving the bacon drippings. Crumble the bacon and set aside.

3. Measure 1/4 cup of bacon drippings and set aside for the dressing.

4. In a few tablespoons of the remaining bacon drippings (use just enough to film the bottom

of the skillet), sauté the chopped onions until tender but not browned.

5. To make the dressing, heat the reserved 1/4 cup bacon drippings in a skillet or saucepan over medium heat until very warm. Sprinkle in the flour, using more flour if a thicker dressing is desired and less for a thinner dressing, and whisk for about 1 minute.

6. Whisk in the hot stock and vinegar, and continue cooking and whisking over low heat until the dressing is smooth and thickened. Add the sugar, salt, pepper, and mustard. Taste for seasoning and correct as needed. The dressing can also be thinned by adding a little warm vinegar and/or stock, if desired.

7. When the potatoes are just tender, drain and peel while still warm. Slice them into a bowl. Add the sautéed onion mixture, the reserved crumbled bacon, and the dressing, tossing gently until the potatoes are well coated and the ingredients are well blended. Serve hot or at room temperature.

Tip: The potatoes are gently boiled with the skin on and then peeled after they are cooked. Use any thin-skinned, waxy potatoes, such as red, Yukon Gold, or White Rose for the best texture. Baking potatoes are more likely to crumble.

Mashed Potato and Cheese Pie

A classic recipe using potato flakes? Yup. My mother came up with this recipe after we complained that mashed potatoes from a box were boring. It's a classic and classy way to prepare a quick, nutritious side dish.

Serves 8

1 (9-inch) pie crust, unbaked

2 cups water

3 tablespoons butter

1/2 teaspoon salt

1/2 teaspoon dried oregano

1/2 teaspoon garlic powder

1/8 teaspoon black pepper

2 1/2 cups potato flakes for instant mashed potatoes

1/2 cup sour cream

6 slices crisp bacon, crumbled

1/2 cup plus 2 tablespoons thinly sliced scallions

4 ounces shredded Cheddar cheese (about 1 cup)

1 tablespoon olive or vegetable oil

1/2 cup sour cream

1. Preheat the oven to 450°F.

2. Line a 9-inch deep-dish or regular pie pan with the pie crust and crimp the edges. Bake for 9 to 11 minutes, or until light golden brown. Cool while preparing the mashed potatoes.

3. Reduce the oven temperature to 400°F.

4. Meanwhile, in a large saucepan, combine the water, butter, salt, oregano, garlic powder, and pepper. Bring to a boil. Remove from the heat and stir in the potato flakes, sour cream, and bacon. Mix well.

5. Sprinkle 1/2 cup of scallions over the bottom of the cooled pie crust, then sprinkle with the cheese. Spoon and spread the mashed potato mixture evenly over the cheese, then brush the top of the mixture with the oil.

6. Bake for 15 to 20 minutes, or until thoroughly heated in the center.

7. Remove from the oven and let cool slightly (about 5 minutes), then sprinkle with the remaining 2 tablespoons scallions.

8. Cut into wedges, top each slice with a spoonful of sour cream, and serve.

Tip: As a variation, spread half the potato mixture in the pie pan, sprinkle shredded Cheddar, feta, or asiago cheese on top, and then cover with the rest of the mashed potatoes.

Gold Potatoes with Roasted Garlic Dressing

This is for people who love garlic. The buttery, nutty flavor of roasted garlic and the rich taste of the Yukon Gold potatoes will win you over. If you wish, you can double the garlic, using two heads instead of one.

Serves 6 to 8

1 head garlic

2 pounds Yukon Gold potatoes

1 teaspoon salt, plus more to taste

2 tablespoons white wine vinegar

1/2 cup chopped red onion

1/3 cup chopped fresh parsley

1/2 cup mayonnaise

Black pepper

1. To roast the garlic, preheat a grill or oven to 350°F.

2. Cut a thin slice off the top of the garlic head, exposing the cloves, then remove the papery white skin from the outside; do not separate the cloves. Wrap in aluminum foil.

3. Bake until the cloves are soft to the touch, about 1 hour. Let the garlic cool for 10 minutes.

4. Separate the cloves and squeeze each one from the root end to extract the garlic pulp from the thin sheaths. Set aside.

5. Put the potatoes in a large saucepan with lots of room and enough water to just cover them. Add 1 teaspoon of salt, cover partially, bring to a boil, and cook until the potatoes are tender when pierced, 20 to 25 minutes. Drain and return to the warm pan, turning with a spatula to dry them. Set aside to cool.

6. When the potatoes are cool enough to handle, peel them and cut into 1/4-inch-thick slices. Place in a large bowl and sprinkle with the vinegar.

7. Add the onions and parsley and set aside until cooled to room temperature.

8. In a small bowl, add 2 or 3 tablespoons of garlic pulp to the mayonnaise and mix, adding salt and pepper to taste.

9. Pour the mayonnaise mixture over the potatoes and mix gently but thoroughly, turning the potatoes over from the bottom with a rubber spatula. Serve immediately, or refrigerate overnight, covered, and serve chilled the next day.

Tip: There are those who add hard-boiled eggs, crumbled bacon, and finely minced dill pickles to this dish. Bravo, I say, but I like this simple recipe unadorned.

Mashed Sweet Taters and Beans

An old Carolina recipe, this unusual dish combines sweet potatoes with tender lima beans and goes extremely well with any pork dish, including ribs, roasts, and ham steaks.

Serves 4 to 6

2 tablespoons olive oil

1 large onion, chopped

2 teaspoons minced garlic

6 cups kidney beans (about 1/2 pound), cooked, rinsed, and drained

1 cup water

3 tablespoons chili powder

1/2 teaspoon ground cloves

4 teaspoons prepared mustard

3 tablespoons brown sugar

Pinch of cayenne pepper

3 tablespoons soy sauce

4 large sweet potatoes

2 tablespoons butter

1/2 pound shredded Cheddar cheese (about 2 cups)

1 cup chopped sweet onion, such as Maui, Walla Walla, or Vidalia

1. Preheat the oven to 350°F.

2. Heat the oil in a medium skillet and sauté the onions and garlic until soft. Add the beans and mash them well with a fork or potato masher.

3. Gradually stir in the water and heat the beans until warmed through. Remove from the heat and stir in the chili powder, cloves, mustard, brown sugar, cayenne pepper, and soy sauce.

4. Wash the sweet potatoes and put them in a saucepan. Add enough water to just cover them and boil for 10 to 12 minutes, or until very soft. Scoop out the insides, discarding the skins.

5. In a large bowl, mash the sweet potatoes with the butter. Pour into a buttered (or sprayed) cast iron skillet. Add the mashed beans, gently stirring into the potatoes until you have a swirl of the two mixtures. Bake for 12 minutes.

6. Serve in the cast iron skillet with the cheese and chopped sweet onion on the side.

Tip: Sweet potatoes spoil rapidly. To keep them fresh, store in a dry, cool (55° to 60°F) place such a cellar, pantry, or garage. Do not store them in the refrigerator, where they will develop a hard core and an "off" taste.

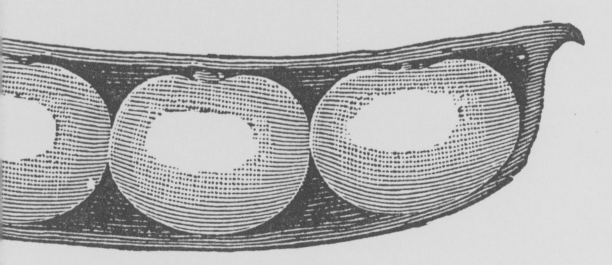

CHAPTER 9 FRUITS

Once eaten mainly by hand, fresh fruit has reappeared on the culinary stage in supporting and even starring roles. Grilled with a touch of rum, curried, or glazed over a stovetop, fruit brings us sweet, tasty, and healthy sides aplenty.

Grilled Fruit Medley

Lots of people love grilled fruit as a side dish or dessert. This recipe is quick to prepare, and the lovely sauce perfectly sets off the fruit. It goes very well with roast chicken and grilled white fish, such as trout or cod.

Serves 4

2 medium tart apples, such as Fuji or Granny Smith, cored and quartered

2 small pears, such as Bosc or Comice, cored and quartered

2 large peaches, pitted and quartered

10 small red plums, pitted and halved

Juice of 1 lemon

3 tablespoons brown sugar

Sauce:

3 large egg yolks

1/4 cup ounces brown sugar

1/2 cup ounces dry cider

1. Preheat the grill to 500°F or hotter.

2. Place the cut fruit in a large bowl and toss with the lemon juice and 2 tablespoons of brown sugar. Reserve any juices that leak out of the fruit.

3. Place the fruit on the hot grill and sprinkle with the remaining tablespoon brown sugar. They will take about 15 to 20 minutes to become caramelized and tinged brown at the edges. As the fruit caramelizes, transfer to a heated platter.

4. Make the sauce by placing the egg yolks and 1/4 cup brown sugar in the top pot of a double boiler and whisk until it starts to thicken. As the sauce thickens, trickle in the cider and reserved fruit juices. Stir continually until the sauce thickens to a fluffy consistency.

5. Drizzle the sauce on the bowl of fruit and reserve any extra in a sealable bottle. Serve the salad while it is still warm. Seal the bottle of sauce and cool to room temperature. It can be stored in the refrigerator for up to one week once it has been opened.

Tip: On the right is a list of fruits you can easily grill.

Fruit and Preparation	Grill Time and Temperature
Apples, whole	35 to 40 minutes (indirect medium)
Apples, cut into 1/2-inch-thick rounds	4 to 6 minutes (direct medium)
Apricots, halved and pitted	6 to 8 minutes (direct medium)
Bananas, cut in half lengthwise	6 to 8 minutes (direct medium)
Cantaloupes, cut into wedges	6 to 8 minutes (direct medium)
Nectarines, halved lengthwise and pitted	8 to 10 minutes (direct medium)
Peaches, halved lengthwise and pitted	8 to 10 minutes (direct medium)
Pears, halved lengthwise	10 to 12 minutes (direct medium)
Pineapples, peeled, cored, and cut into 1/2-inch-thick rings or cut lengthwise into 1-inch-thick wedges	5 to 10 minutes (direct medium)
Strawberries, whole and skewered	4 to 5 minutes (direct medium)

Classic Grilled Grapefruit

During the Great Depression, lots of people "made do," and that meant finding inexpensive foods to cook. With lots of fresh grapefruit available in Florida, folks there discovered this spiced and quite tasty dessert literally hanging in their backyards.

Serves 4

3 large grapefruit (preferably from Florida)

1 tablespoon sugar

1/2 teaspoon ground cinnamon

1. Preheat a grill to medium-high. Slice the ends off the grapefruit.

2. Cut the grapefruit into 3/4-inch-thick rounds, yielding 3 or 4 slices each. Combine the sugar and cinnamon. Sprinkle the sugar mixture on both sides of each slice.

3. Grill the grapefruit for 5 minutes, or until the slices are hot and the sugar begins to caramelize. Make sure to turn the slices halfway through cooking. Serve hot.

Tip: For a tasty dessert, grill as described, then mix 1/4 cup warm rum with 1/4 cup brown sugar and stir until the sugar dissolves. Pour the mixture onto the grilled grapefruit just before you bring it to the table, and light each slice with a charcoal lighter. Presto— grapefruit flambé!

Grilled Plantains with Spicy Glaze

Plantains are a staple food in the tropical regions of the world, treated in much the same way as potatoes and with a similar neutral flavor and texture when unripe. Green plantains are firm and starchy, yellow plantains are slightly sweeter, and extremely ripe plantains are black, with a soft, very sweet, deep yellow pulp. This dish is a bit of the tropics on a plate—the citrus juices and allspice reminiscent of Jamaica, the plantains of Hawaii. All together they make a very fresh and tangy dish.

Serves 4

4 very ripe plantains, peeled and sliced diagonally (1/2-inch-thick slices)

2 tablespoons vegetable oil

1/4 cup light brown sugar

2 tablespoons orange juice

1 teaspoon lime juice

1 tablespoon honey

1/2 teaspoon ground allspice

2 tablespoons chopped fresh parsley

Salt and pepper

1. Preheat the grill to medium-high (350° to 400°F).

2. Brush the plantains with the oil and grill until caramelized, about 2 minutes on each side.

3. In a small bowl, combine the brown sugar, juices, honey, allspice, and parsley. Season to taste with salt and pepper.

4. Remove the plantains to a heated platter and pour the glaze over the top.

5. Keep the platter and fruit warm in the oven or in indirect heat on the grill until you are ready to serve.

Tip: Plantains are a wonderful side dish to accompany grilled or baked fish, grilled chicken, shrimp or grilled scallops.

Jack Daniel's Peachtarines

Distilled and bottled in the tiny town of Lynchburg, Tennessee, Jack Daniel's is one of the finest "sippin' whiskies" in America.

Best y'all be servin' this side dish with smoked country ham or succulent butter-flied leg of lamb.

Serves 4

1 pound peaches, peeled, pitted, and quartered

1 pound nectarines, peeled, pitted, and quartered

2 cups packed brown sugar

2 cups water

1/2 cup plus 2 tablespoons Jack Daniel's

1 cinnamon stick

Dash of ground nutmeg

1. In a heavy saucepan, combine the peaches, nectarines, sugar, water, 1/2 cup of Jack Daniel's, and cinnamon stick. Bring the mixture to a rolling boil, then reduce the heat to softly boil the fruit until it can be pierced easily but is not too soft, about 5 minutes.

2. Remove the pan from the heat, discard the cinnamon stick, and pour the fruit and syrup into a sealable container to the top so no air gets to the fruit. You can also weigh the fruit down with a small bowl so it stays under the syrup. Refrigerate for at least 12 hours.

3. Just before serving, add the remaining 2 tablespoons Jack Daniel's and stir to mix well. Serve at room temperature with sprinkled nutmeg.

Tip: Instead of a cinnamon stick, try using a whole vanilla bean for extra flavor.

Savory Applesauce

Homemade applesauce brings back memories of my mother in the kitchen with steaming pots of delicious apples, sugar, butter, and spices. This simple applesauce, with some golden raisins added, is wonderful with 2-inch-thick pork chops, as a side dish with turkey breast, or on waffles.

Serves 4 to 6

1 cup dry white wine

1/4 cup port wine

3 1/2 pounds tart apples, such as Granny Smith, peeled (reserve 1/2 cup of peels)

Juice of 1 lemon

1/4 cup butter

1 teaspoon ground cinnamon

2/3 cup sugar

1 cup golden raisins

1/2 teaspoon salt

1. Combine the wine and port in a small saucepan and cook over medium-high heat until reduced by half, about 5 minutes.

2. While the wine is reducing, quarter and core the apples. Roughly chop in batches in a food processor, pulsing to prevent over-processing and adding the 1/2 cup reserved peels to one batch. Place all the apples in a deep stockpot and set aside.

3. Place the saucepan containing the reduced wine-port mixture over medium heat and add the lemon juice, butter, cinnamon, sugar, raisins, and salt. Stir until the sugar dissolves, about 5 minutes.

4. Pour the wine-port mixture over the chopped apples and stir until well combined.

5. Place the stockpot on the burner, cover the pot, and simmer until the apples are tender, 25 to 30 minutes, stirring every few minutes. Serve warm or at room temperature.

Tip: Do not, under any circumstances, make applesauce from "special" apples given to you by a haggard old woman standing beside a tiny seven-bedroom cottage in the woods near a castle in a kingdom far away. Stick with Granny Smith apples, or use Pippin apples as an alternative.

Chilled Raspberry-Mango-Peach Bisque

Native Americans used wild raspberries all year long, eating them fresh in the summer and drying them in cakes to eat in the winter months. They used the leaves and roots for medicinal purposes as well. This bisque is extremely refreshing and cooling on a hot summer's evening.

Serves 4

1 1/2 cups orange juice

2 pints raspberries

2 cups puréed mango

2 medium bananas, peeled

2 medium peaches, peeled and pitted

1 cup milk or half-and-half

3 tablespoons heavy cream

Whipped cream, to serve

Sprigs of fresh mint, to serve

1. In a large blender, combine the orange juice, raspberries, mango, bananas, peaches, milk, and heavy cream. Purée until smooth.

2. Store in the refrigerator until ready to serve. Pour the chilled soup into bowls and serve with a dollop of whipped cream and a sprig of fresh mint as a garnish.

Tip: Since berries are notorious for staining your clothing, here's a secret. Heat a teakettle filled with water to a full boil, stretch the stained fabric over a large bowl, and pour the hot water directly onto the stain. Repeat until the stain vanishes.

Baked Peaches and Blueberries

Grilled fruit adds a nice touch to roasted meats, fish, and poultry. Replace starch dishes with fresh fruits for a healthy and flavorful meal that is easy to prepare and will surprise most of your guests. This bright dish of orange and blue livens up any picnic or luncheon table, and the mix of textures and flavors is quite surprising.

Serves 4

4 large peaches

1 pint fresh or frozen blueberries (about 2 cups)

4 tablespoons brown sugar

4 tablespoons lemon juice

4 pinches of ground cloves

1. Preheat a grill to 350°F. Wash and halve the peaches, removing the pits, then place each half on a double thickness of heavy-duty aluminum foil that you've sprayed with nonstick cooking spray.

2. Fill the peach halves generously with the blueberries. Sprinkle a tablespoon of brown sugar and lemon juice on each, then add a pinch of ground cloves to each (just a pinch, though, as too much will overpower the fruit flavors).

3. Wrap the fruit securely, sealing the foil packages well, and grill for 15 to 20 minutes without turning over.

4. With a spatula, remove the peach halves from the foil and place them, open side up, on individual plates. Serve immediately.

Tip: These grilled peaches are magnificent served with sliced ham steaks, grilled chicken breasts, or barbecued pork chops.

Grilled Avocado with Strawberry-Mango Salsa

There are more than 80 varieties of the avocado fruit, with the Hass variety responsible for 85 percent of production. The Hass avocado was discovered by a California postman named Rudolf Hass. Avocados are rich in unsaturated fats, contain no cholesterol, and are packed with dietary fiber and vitamins such as folic acid, A, B6, C, thiamin, and riboflavin. And for good measure, this salsa adds honey, mango, strawberries, and citrus juices to complete the healthy affair.

Serves 4

4 medium avocados, just turning soft, not fully ripe

1/4 cup honey

1/4 cup olive oil

1 medium mango, peeled, pitted, and cut into 1/2-inch cubes

1/2 pound strawberries (about 1 cup), hulled and cut into 1/2-inch cubes

1 tablespoon balsamic vinegar

1/3 cup orange juice

2 tablespoons lemon juice

Leaves of lettuce, such as romaine or iceberg, to serve

1. Preheat a well-oiled grill to medium-high, 300° to 400°F.

2. Slice the avocados in half lengthwise, and carefully remove the pit; do not peel them. In a small bowl, mix the honey with the oil.

Brush the exposed avocado flesh with this mixture, cover with plastic wrap and set aside in a cool place (do not refrigerate).

3. In a medium bowl, mix the mango and strawberries with the vinegar, orange juice, and lemon juice. Let the mixture rest for at least 20 minutes, stirring occasionally, so the flavors can blend.

4. Grill the avocados, skin side down, for 2 to 3 minutes, until the skin begins to lightly char and take on grill marks. Brush the flesh side of the avocados again with the honey-oil mixture and place them, flesh side down, on the hot grill for another 2 or 3 minutes.

5. With a spatula, carefully remove the avocados from the grill and place on a bed of lettuce on a serving plate, 2 halves per person. Fill the seed cavity with mango-strawberry salsa, generously dribbling some on top of each half. Serve with a spoon to scoop out the avocado flesh and salsa.

Tip: Do not store unripe fruit in the refrigerator. To ripen avocados, place them in a brown paper bag at room temperature for 2 to 5 days, keeping them away from direct sunlight. To hurry up the ripening process, add an apple or a banana to the bag.

Fijian Barbecued Pineapple

Choose nice, fresh pineapples that are golden in color, have a pleasant sweet scent, and are firm to the touch. Save the top of the pineapple, with the sharp leaves attached, to use as a garnish for the bowl of cooked pineapple. Fresh pineapple mixed with rum, brown sugar, and butter —who needs ice cream or chocolate cake? This is pure indulgence.

Serves 4 to 6

2 tablespoons Worcestershire sauce

1/2 cup (1 stick) butter

1/2 cup packed dark brown sugar

1/2 cup dark rum

Pinch of salt

Pinch of black pepper

1 large pineapple, cored and cut into 8 vertical wedges or sliced into 1/2-inch-thick circles

1. Combine the Worcestershire sauce, butter, sugar, and rum in a medium saucepan. Add the salt and pepper, then bring the liquid to a boil, stirring constantly.

2. Reduce the heat and simmer until the sauce begins to thicken, about 10 minutes. Remove from the heat and allow to cool.

3. Preheat a grill to 400°F and oil it. Brush the pineapple pieces with the cooled sauce and place on the grill over the flame. Cook for about 5 minutes, turning occasionally, until the pineapple browns nicely on all sides.

4. Remove from the grill and serve, cautioning guests about the very hot pineapple juices and sugars.

Tip: This is fantastic with roasted chicken, or with white-meat fish steaks or fillets. You can omit the Worcestershire sauce if you wish.

Classic

Tri-Color Gelatin Salad

This three-layer fruit salad is made in a glass bread or loaf pan. You can vary the colors by using grape, cherry, orange, strawberry, or black cherry gelatin.

Serves 4 to 6

1 (3-ounce) package cherry gelatin, such as Jell-O

3 cups boiling water

1 cup juice from canned pears

6 canned pear halves

6 maraschino cherries

1 (3-ounce) package lemon gelatin, such as Jell-O

1 cup cold water

1 cup heavy cream

1 (8-ounce) package cream cheese, softened

1 (3-ounce) package lime gelatin, such as Jell-O

1 cup orange juice

1 (11-ounce) can mandarin orange segments, drained

1. In a medium bowl, dissolve the cherry gelatin in 1 cup of boiling water and add the pear juice. Place the pear halves in 2 glass loaf pans (3 in each pan down the center), cut sides down, and place a cherry in the hollow of each pear. Pour the gelatin over the pears and put in the refrigerator to jell.

2. In a medium bowl, dissolve the lemon gelatin in 1 cup of boiling water and add the cold water. Let thicken slightly in the refrigerator. Whip the cream and fold it into the gelatin. Mix in the cream cheese and pour over the red layer in the loaf pans. Chill until set.

3. In a medium bowl, dissolve the lime gelatin in the remaining 1 cup boiling water and add the orange juice. Stir in the mandarin oranges and pour over the cream cheese layer. Chill until set.

4. To unmold a salad, dip the loaf pan into hot water for 30 seconds, place a plate over the top, invert, and tap on the bottom of the pan. The molded gelatin should slip right out onto the plate; the red layer will be on top, the white in the center, and the green at the bottom. Unmold the second loaf pan and serve immediately.

Tip: Gelatin salads were huge in the 1950s. Just about any flavor of gelatin, with fruit (grapes raspberries, bananas, cherries, etc.) and cream cheese added, along with a whipped cream garnish, made it to our tables.

Curried Fruit

This is a great side dish for thick ham slices or grilled leg of lamb. The fruit adds a nice softness to a meal of heavy meat and is a very colorful addition to any plate.

Serves 6 to 8

1 (15-ounce) can pear halves, drained

1 (15-ounce) can peach halves, drained

2 (16-ounce) cans apricot halves, drained

1 (15-ounce) can pineapple chunks, drained

1 cup firmly packed brown sugar

1 tablespoon curry powder

1/2 cup (1 stick) butter, melted

1 (20-ounce) can pineapple slices, drained

1 (4-ounce) jar maraschino cherries, drained

1. Place the pears, peaches, apricots, and pineapple chunks in a large pot or Dutch oven, and stir to mix.

2. Add the brown sugar, curry powder, and butter and cover.

3. Cook for 1 hour on low heat, stirring occasionally.

4. Serve as a side dish, placing a pineapple slice on each serving and filling the hole in the slice with a maraschino cherry.

Tip: You can add 1/2 cup of cashews, almonds, pistachio nuts, roasted peanuts, or pine nuts just before serving to add a little crunch to this dish. By the way, fresh fruit doesn't work as well as the canned in this recipe.

Stovetop Glazed Pears

Serve these cooked pears warm to accompany roasted or grilled meat. The mild sweet-and-sour taste makes a great side dish for prime rib or crown roast of pork or lamb.

Serves 8

1/4 cup concentrated lemon juice

2 cups water

16 medium pears, unpeeled, cored, and sliced lengthwise in wedges

2 tablespoons butter

1/4 cup packed dark brown sugar

Juice of 2 lemons

1. In a large bowl, add the lemon juice to the water.

2. Place the pears in the water for 10 to 15 minutes, to prevent them from turning brown. Drain and pat them dry with paper towels. Set aside.

3. Melt the butter in a large sauté pan and add the pears, cut side down. Cook over medium heat for about 10 minutes.

4. Turn the pears over and sprinkle with the brown sugar. Continue cooking until the juices reduce. Watch that the pears glaze and do not burn.

5. After 2 to 3 minutes, sprinkle the pears with the fresh lemon juice and cook for a few more minutes. Serve immediately.

Tip: You can use one variety of pears in this dish, or try mixing d'Anjous, red d'Anjous, Boscs, and Bartletts together. A touch of nutmeg (1/4 teaspoon) can add a nice bit of flavor as well.

Grilled Cantaloupe

Grilling brings out the juicy flavors of most fruit, and melons respond particularly well to a quick grilling. The honey and lemon in this recipe add a sweet tang, and the pepper a bit of a bite. You can also serve this as an appetizer.

Serves 4

1/4 cup honey

1/4 cup lemon juice

1 large cantaloupe

Black pepper

1. Preheat a grill to high. Mix the honey and lemon juice in a flat dish.

2. Cut the cantaloupe into 1/2-inch round slices, then remove the seeds and cut the slices in half so you have half-moons.

3. Dip both sides of the slices into the honey-lemon mixture.

4. Place the coated slices on the hot grill and cook just long enough to get good grill marks on both sides of the melon.

5. Place the cantaloupe on a serving platter and generously sprinkle black pepper over both sides of the slices. Serve warm as a side dish with pork chops, halibut steaks or fillets, or grilled chicken breasts.

Tip: You want melons that are firm, not ripe and soft. Also, you can use any flavored honey.

2 tablespoons lemon juice

1 cup finely chopped celery

1/2 cup broken or coarsely chopped walnuts

1 cup halved seedless grapes (red and/or green), or 1 cup golden raisins

1/4 cup mayonnaise

2 tablespoons half-and-half

4 leaves lettuce, such as romaine or iceberg

1. Wash and core the apples. Do not peel.

2. Dice the apples and, in a medium bowl, toss with the lemon juice to prevent browning. Refrigerate while preparing the other ingredients.

3. Mix the celery, walnuts, and grapes in a medium bowl, then add the apples and stir to combine.

4. Blend in the mayonnaise and half-and-half until well mixed. Cover tightly and chill thoroughly. Serve chilled, placing a large scoop on a cold lettuce leaf on each plate.

Tip: For a spicier salad, you can add 1/8 teaspoon ground allspice with the other ingredients before refrigerating. Just make sure you stir it in well.

Waldorf Salad

This is perhaps America's most classic fruit salad. Created at New York's Waldorf-Astoria Hotel in 1896 by maître d'hôtel Oscar Tschirky, the Waldorf salad was an instant success. The original version of this salad contained only apples, celery, and mayonnaise. Chopped walnuts later became an integral part of the dish.

Serves 4

4 medium apples, such as Red and/or Golden Delicious

INDEX